Christmas
in Colorado
Cook Book

edited

by

Marie Cahill

GOLDEN
WEST ✷
PUBLISHERS

Cover photo by Dick Dietrich

Acknowledgements

The editor would like to thank all the Colorado cooks who shared their recipes and their Christmas memories; the Colorado Historical Society; American National CattleWomen; Four Mile Historic Park; Historic Georgetown; and Bent's Old Fort National Historic Site. She would also like to express her gratitude to Jeanne Cahill and Margaret Palmer for their recipe contributions, and offer special thanks to Thora Cahill for her editorial assistance.

Printed in the United States of America

ISBN #0-914846-84-1

Second Printing ©1995

Golden West Publishers, Inc.
4113 N. Longview Ave.
Phoenix, AZ 85014, USA
(602) 265-4392

Christmas in Colorado Cook Book

Table of Contents

A Sampling of Christmas Events in Colorado

Alamosa—Christmas Lighting Festival

Aspen—Hotel Jerome, 1889 Opening Celebration; Snowmass Torchlight Parade down Fanny Hill with Santa

Beulah—Yule Log Hunt

Boulder—University of Colorado, Boulder Philharmonic Orchestra, *The Nutcracker*

Breckenridge—Lighting of Breckenridge; Old Fashioned Christmas Home Tour

Colorado Springs—The Broadmoor Annual White Light Tree Lighting Ceremony; Colorado Springs Symphony, Winter Springs Fantasy; Festival of Lights Tree Lighting and Parade; Old Colorado City, Old Fashioned Christmas.

Copper Mountain—Christmas Eve Torchlight Parade and Fireworks

Cortez—Parade of Lights

Denver—World's Largest Christmas Lighting Display; Parade of Lights; Buffalo Bill's Holiday Celebration; Denver Zoo, Wild Lights; Colorado Children's Chorale, Christmas Concerts, Colorado Symphony Orchestra; Denver Botanic Gardens, Blossoms of Light; Lighting of the Denver City and County Building

Durango—A Durango Christmas—How They Did It In 1891

Estes Park—Christmas Parade; Estes Park Music Festival, Colorado Children's Chorale

Georgetown—Christmas Market; Christmas at Hammill House

Glenwood Springs—Luminaria Lighting Celebration and Candlelight Holiday Walk

Greeley—Festival of Trees

Gunnison—Christmas Parade and Christmas Tree Lighting

Keystone—Cross Country Moonlight tour

Pueblo—Rosemount Victorian Christmas, *A Dickens of a Christmas*; El Pueblo Museum, Living Christmas of the 1840's

Steamboat Springs—Howelsen Hill, Annual Christmas Town Party

Telluride—Winter Jazz Festival/Winter Festival Series; The Telluride Museum, Victorian Christmas

Vail/Beaver Creek—Festival of Lights; Crystal Ball; Annual Holiday Fair; Annual Tree Lightings at Vail, Beaver Creek and Lionshead

Winter Park—Christmas Eve Torchlight Parade

Colorado at a Glance

❋ **Colorado was admitted to the Union on August 1, 1876, becoming the 38th state.** Its name comes from the Spanish word for red—the color the Spanish explorers used to describe the Colorado River.

❋ **It is the eighth largest state in the nation,** encompassing over 104,000 square miles.

❋ **The state's highest point is Mt. Elbert** at 14,433 feet.

❋ **State Nickname:** Centennial State

❋ **State Motto:** Nil Sine Numine (Nothing Without Providence)

❋ **State Capital:** Denver

❋ **State Flower:** White and lavender columbine

❋ **State Gem:** Aquamarine

❋ **State Animal:** Rocky Mountain Bighorn Sheep

❋ **State Tree:** Blue Spruce

❋ **State Bird:** Lark Bunting

The following article appeared in the Rocky Mountain News, Dec. 25, 1903, p.10

CHRISTMAS FLOWERS ARE VERY PLENTIFUL IN DENVER THIS YEAR!

American Beauty Roses, Violets, Carnations, Ferns, Holly and Many other varieties of Yuletide Evergreens Imported by Local Florists in Carload Lots from the Greenhouses of Texas, Alabama and Southern States

Sweet chimes are ringing everywhere
The world is glad today
The Yuletide log is burning bright
And flowers bedeck our way

Flowers at Christmas time seem to bud and burst into fragrant bloom, as if impelled by the magic of the earth, bearing from their tender petals their share of good cheer and sacred memories to the old home, the old associates, the fireplace and the yuletide season of happy days of youth.

Denver's supply of flowers, rich green foliage, red-berried holly, clinging smilax and interlacing vines and draperies, was never more ample than this year. Although this is the midwinter season and every flower has, of necessity, to be artificially bred, nature could not surpass the product of the floriculturist's art as displayed today.

Days and days ago little girls and feeble old women began selling their wreaths of dyed everlastings, holly and Christmas roping. Weeks and weeks ago the florists began their careful preparation for the yuletide festivities. To satisfy the great demand for holly and mistletoe, orders were sent to Alabama, Oklahoma and Texas for carloads of the beautiful green stuff. From the greenhouses out of town were brought thousands of pots of azaleas, cyclamen, poinsettias, asparagus ferns and Boston ferns all of which are sold in case quantities for decoration.

CHAPTER ONE

Christmas in Colorado

Christmas, perhaps more so than any other holiday, is tradition. The Christmas season is filled with customs, some that have been passed down from generation to generation, some of a more recent vintage. Like families across the United States, families in Colorado have special customs and rituals associated with this most magical time of the year. For many families it's the annual pilgrimage to see the *Nutcracker* or a small town production of Dickens' *A Christmas Carol* or hear the glorious strains of Handel's *Messiah* performed by the Colorado Symphony. Others will find themselves romping through the snow to find that perfect tree, or visiting Aunt Evelyn to sample her delicious pecan pie. Christmas Eve may call for roasting tiny hot dogs or watching *It's a Wonderful Life* for the two hundredth time.

At Christmas time, Colorado becomes a winter wonderland, and outdoor activities are a natural way to savor the state's breathtaking beauty. Many head to the slopes to spend the holidays skiing. Others enjoy Christmas caroling with friends and family, followed by a warm cup of Mexican Hot Chocolate. For Sharon Galligar Chance and Don Chance of Colorado Springs, Christmas means taking their four boys sledding over Christmas vacation.

"We pick a sunny day to drive up to Lake Manitou," writes Sharon, "and take along a winter picnic. The boys have a blast scooting down the hills, and are more than ready for a hearty bowl of chili when it's time to eat. At sundown we pack up and head back down to Colorado Springs, and drive around looking at the beautiful Christmas light displays.

"The sights of Christmas in Colorado Springs are wondrous to behold, from the grandly decorated Victorian houses, to the millions of tiny white lights which adorn the Broadmoor Hotel, to the fanciful decorations which light the downtown area. Colorado Springs truly becomes a Christmas Wonderland. Christmas in Colorado Springs is a magical experience, one that is forever treasured in our family's memories."

A Rocky Mountain Winter Picnic

Sharon Galligar Chance

1 lg. thermos of HOT CHOCOLATE WITH TINY MARSHMALLOWS
1 cooler with a 6-pack of SODAS (in case the hot chocolate is too hot!)
1 kettle of BUBBLING HOT CHILI ON AN OPEN CAMPFIRE
1 pan of fresh, sweet CORNBREAD
A couple of nice, soft old QUILTS TO SIT ON (the picnic benches will be cold)
4 hungry little BOYS, fresh in from sledding

Mix well with a good dose of winter sunshine and beautiful mountain surroundings.

Yield: Years and years of memories

Beverages

Many Colorado families are delighted by the spectacle of lights at the Broadmoor. Nestled at the foothills of the Rocky Mountains, this famed hotel was built in 1918 by self-made millionaire Spencer Penrose. Today a world renowned resort, at Christmas time the Broadmoor is host to various holiday events such as puppet shows and Christmas concerts, but many people go to the Broadmoor just to enjoy its old world ambience and to toast the season with a cup of Wassail punch.

Cider Wassail Bowl

A Wassail Bowl is an old Christmas tradition that began in England. Christmas revelers would gather round the Wassail bowl and raise a toast. The word wassail means "to your good health." This recipe, provided courtesy of the Broadmoor in Colorado Springs and Chef Siegfried Eisenberger, was originally from Scandinavia.

1 lg. tart APPLE, cored and cut into slices
1 tsp. LEMON JUICE
1/4 cup + 1 tsp. BROWN SUGAR
1 tsp. unsalted BUTTER or MARGARINE
1 qt. APPLE CIDER
1 tsp. grated LEMON ZEST
1 tsp. grated ORANGE ZEST
1 tsp. whole CARDAMOM PODS
6 ALLSPICE BERRIES
1 CINNAMON STICK, broken in half
6 whole CLOVES
1/2 cup DARK RUM
1/2 cup APPLE BRANDY
1 can (12 oz.) LIGHT ALE
1/4 tsp. grated NUTMEG

Preheat the oven to 300 degrees. Toss the apple slices in lemon juice. Arrange them in a shallow baking pan in a single layer and sprinkle with 1 teaspoon of the brown sugar and dot with butter or margarine. Bake for about 20 minutes or until the apples are tender. Let cool slightly.

(Continued next page)

Bring the cider, lemon and orange zests and the remaining 1/4 cup brown sugar to a boil over high heat in a large pot, stirring to dissolve the sugar. Tie the cardamom, allspice, cinnamon and cloves in a cheese cloth and add to the cider mixture. Cover and simmer over low heat for 20 minutes. Add the rum, apple brandy and ale and return to a simmer. Remove from the heat and discard the spice bag. Pour the cider into a punch bowl. Garnish with apple slices and sprinkle with the nutmeg. Serve hot in punch cups or small mugs.

Serves 12.

Wassail Punch

Donald Gleason of Pueblo makes a non-alcoholic version of the classic Wassail punch. His version was inspired by the punch served at the annual Beulah, Colorado Yule Log Festival. Each December for over 40 years, the Yule Log Festival is held in Pueblo Mountain Park, starting at Horseshoe Lodge in Beulah. The search is on for the Yule log, hidden in the park. The finder gets a ride back to the Lodge on the log, where they serve Wassail Punch.

1 cup GRAPEFRUIT JUICE	1/4 cup SUGAR
2 1/2 cups ORANGE JUICE	6 whole CLOVES
2 cups APPLE CIDER	1 CINNAMON STICK,
1/2 cup WATER	broken

Combine juice, cider and water in bottom of clean 12 cup coffee maker. Put sugar and spices in coffee maker basket. Perk until signal light indicates punch is ready. Remove spices and serve from coffee maker.

Cranberry Punch

"This colorful punch adds sparkle and color to any gathering for Christmas." Donald Gleason, Pueblo

2/3 cup SUGAR
1 6-inch CINNAMON STICK, broken
2 tsp. whole ALLSPICE
1 to 2 tsp. whole CLOVES
1/4 tsp. SALT
1 qt. CRANBERRY JUICE COCKTAIL
2 1/2 cups unsweetened PINEAPPLE JUICE
1 bottle (28 ozs.) GINGER ALE
ORANGE SLICES

Combine sugar, spices, salt, cranberry juice and pineapple juice. Cover and simmer gently for 10 minutes. Strain. Chill. Just before serving, pour ginger ale down side of bowl. Float orange slices on top of punch.
Yield: 3 quarts.

Rocky Mountain Bloody Mary

A wonderful eye opener for a New Year's Day Brunch.

1 bottle (28 oz.) TOMATO JUICE
1 Tbsp. HORSERADISH
Juice from 1/2 LEMON
1/2 tsp. RED PEPPER
1/2 tsp. GARLIC POWDER
Dash CELERY SALT
Dash freshly ground BLACK PEPPER
TABASCO® to taste
VODKA to taste
LIMES, quartered

Combine all ingredients except vodka and limes. Stir well. Add vodka if desired and garnish with a lime quarter.

Hot Mulled Wine

1 liter dry RED TABLE WINE
2 CINNAMON STICKS,
    broken in half
1 tsp. ALLSPICE

1 tsp. NUTMEG
1 tsp. CLOVES
1 tsp. GINGER
ORANGE SLICES

Add spices to wine and heat over low heat. Serve in a punch glass with a slice of orange.

Eggnog

1/2 cup SUGAR
1/4 tsp. CINNAMON
1/8 tsp. NUTMEG
dash ALLSPICE

3 EGGS, separated
2 cups MILK
1 cup LIGHT CREAM

Combine first four ingredients. Beat egg whites with electric mixer at high speed until soft peaks form. Slowly beat in half of sugar mixture until stiff peaks form. In small bowl beat yolks until lemon colored. Thoroughly fold into whites. Stir in milk and cream well. Serve well chilled with a sprinkle of **nutmeg**. If desired, add 1/2 shot of **brandy** to each serving.

Rum Stone Sour

For a festive holiday drink, try this delicious concoction.

1 1/2 ozs. freshly squeezed LEMON JUICE
1 1/2 ozs. freshly squeezed ORANGE JUICE
1 Tbsp. SUGAR
1 1/2 ozs. RUM (or VODKA or GIN)

Blend all ingredients and serve on the rocks in an old-fashioned cocktail glass.

Serves 1.

CHAPTER TWO

Los Pastores & Las Posadas

In their exploration of the New World, by the 1700s the Spanish had made their way north from Mexico to southern Colorado. One of the most famous expeditions was led by two Franciscan priests, Francisco Dominguez and Silvestre Escalante, in 1776. They explored the area of the San Juan Mountains, the Dolores River and the Gunnison River, ultimately heading west toward Utah before turning back to Sante Fe. But it wasn't until 1851 that San Luis, Colorado's first permanent non-Indian settlement, was founded by six Hispanic families. The town's Hispanic heritage is reflected to this day in the Christmas time celebrations of *Los Pastores* and *Las Posadas*.

Los Pastores (The Shepherds) is a mystery play that has its roots in medieval times. In medieval Spain, the play was used as a teaching tool in an era when few were literate. In the New World, the Franciscan priests used the play to introduce the Native Americans to Christianity. The plot follows the shepherds en route to Bethlehem to visit El Niño Jesus, the Christ Child. As they make their journey, Lucifer and his followers try to stop them. Ultimately, good triumphs over evil when St. Michael strikes down the devil. Various performances of Los Pastores can be enjoyed throughout southern Colorado and the Southwest.

Las Posadas is another Mexican-Spanish tradition that is looked forward to with anticipation every year at Christmas. Los Posadas, which means "The Inns" is a recreation of Joseph and Mary's search for lodging on the night of Christ's birth. The custom was first introduced in the United

States by Father Diego de Soria in the sixteenth century. Originally, the ritual took place over nine days (a novena) from December 16th through the 24th with nine families participating.

Guided by candlelight, one family would go to the home of the other families, seeking lodging as Joseph and Mary had done. Playing the part of Joseph, the head of the family would sing his request, "Mary my wife is expecting a child. She must have shelter tonight. Let us in. Let us in." The "innkeeper" would answer in song, "I do not trust you go away. Go away."

The next family would follow and so on until eight families had reached the ninth house. This family invited everyone in and the celebrating began. On the ensuing nights the entire ritual would be repeated, each time with a different family playing host.

Today the ritual is generally condensed into one evening, and at the evening's conclusion friends and family gather together for food and drink.

May Your Christmas be a Happy One And may the New Year bring You Contentment and Prosperity in overflowing measure.

Appetizers

Christmas Party Scrabble

Sharon Galligar Chance of Colorado Springs remembers her mother making this zesty party mix at Christmas time when she was a little girl. She now makes it for her own children and it has become a Christmas specialty at her house.

1 box each CHEERIOS®, WHEAT CHEX®, RICE CHEX®
1 sm. bag PRETZEL STICKS
2 cups SALTED PEANUTS
2 cups PECANS
3/4 cup VEGETABLE OIL
1 1/2 sticks MARGARINE
3 Tbsp. WORCESTERSHIRE SAUCE
2 Tbsp. TABASCO®
2 Tbsp. SEASONED SALT
1 Tbsp. PAPRIKA

Combine the dry ingredients in a large paper sack. Over a low flame, combine the remaining ingredients. Bring to a boil, let cool slightly and pour over dry ingredients in sack and shake well. Pour the entire mixture into a roasting pan and bake at 225 degrees for 1 1/2 hours, stirring every half hour. Cool and enjoy.

Yield: approximately 2 gallons of party mix.

Irish Mix

To add color to your Christmas table, try a little Irish Mix. The salty peanuts and the sweet candy make a pleasing contrast of tastes.

1 can REDSKINS or COCKTAIL PEANUTS
1 bag multicolored JELLY GUM DROPS

Mix in equal portions and serve in your most festive candy dish.

Popcorn Crazy Crunch

"This is a good food that young people can help to make and then leave out for Santa Claus on Christmas Eve. At our home, Santa Claus had a hole in his toy bag and so dropped shelled peanuts from the road to the house, inside to the stockings, and out again. The first one up found the peanuts."
Marjorie J. Gleason, Pueblo

2 qts. popped POPCORN
1 1/3 cups PECANS
2/3 cups ALMONDS
1 1/3 cups SUGAR
1/2 cups LIGHT CORN SYRUP
1 cup MARGARINE
1 tsp. VANILLA

Mix popcorn, pecans and almonds in a wide container, similar to bottom of a roasting pan. Combine sugar, corn syrup, and margarine in heavy saucepan — 1 1/2 quart size or more. Bring to boil over medium heat, stirring constantly. Boil to soft ball stage when a little bit of mixture is tested in a little cold water. Remove from heat and add vanilla. Pour over the popcorn and nut mixture. Mix well. Spread mixture to dry. Break into pieces and store in tightly covered container.

Yield: 2 pounds.

Cocktail Balls

A delightful appetizer for any gathering on the holidays.

1 lb. SHARP CHEDDAR CHEESE, grated
1 lb. HOT SAUSAGE
3 cups BISQUICK®

Keep both sausage and cheese at room temperature. Mix together cheese and sausage. Add Bisquick and mix well. Shape into small balls. Place flat in a baking pan and bake at 350 degrees for 20 minutes. Serve warm.

Yield: 35 or 40 balls.

Note: These freeze and reheat well.

Baked Brie with Pesto

Delicious, easy to make—and the green adds a nice holiday touch.

1 round BRIE CHEESE
1 container ready-made PESTO

Place brie on an oven-proof plate and bake at 400 degrees for 5 minutes, or until brie is warm. Pour pesto over the top of the brie. Serve with French bread or crackers.

Buttery Salmon Spread

1/2 cup melted BUTTER,
  room temperature
1 can (7 1/2 oz.) RED SALMON
1 Tbsp. LEMON JUICE

1 tsp. TABASCO®
1 tsp. DIJON MUSTARD
1/2 cup SOUR CREAM

Pureé all ingredients, except sour cream, in a food processor or blender. Stir in sour cream. Chill. Serve with melba toast or water crackers.

Roasted Garlic

Here's a quick and easy spread for garlic lovers. The cooked garlic is smooth and creamy, and spreads like butter.

1 head GARLIC
1 tsp. OLIVE OIL
SALT and PEPPER to taste

Cut a thin slice off the top of the garlic. Pour olive oil over entire head of garlic and sprinkle with salt and pepper. Wrap in aluminum foil and bake in a 400 degree oven for approximately 45 minutes to an 1 hour, or until garlic is soft. Squeeze the cloves onto French bread, taking care not to burn your fingers.

Hot Artichoke Spread

1/2 cup slivered ALMONDS
1 can (14-oz.) ARTICHOKE HEARTS, drained and chopped
1/2 cup grated PARMESAN CHEESE
1/2 cup SOUR CREAM

Toast almonds for 10 minutes at 350 degrees. Mix all ingredients in 1-quart baking dish, reserving some almonds to sprinkle on top. Bake at 350 degrees for 20 minutes.

Serve as spread for crackers or French bread. Recipe can be doubled.

The Queen Anne Bed & Breakfast Inn in Denver treats its guests to a bottomless nut jar. These two recipes were created by Jo Tweed, the Assistant Innkeeper.

Crunchy & Sweet Pecans

1 cup PECAN HALVES
3 cups WATER
3 Tbsp. BROWN SUGAR
PEANUT OIL

Bring water to boil and add nuts; return to boil for one minute. Drain nuts and rinse with warm water. Mix with brown sugar. Heat peanut oil (enough to cover pan bottom); add nuts to peanut oil and stir until nuts are lightly browned. Pour onto wax paper until cool.

Serves 4 - 6, and keeps up to two weeks.

Crunchy & Savory Almonds

1/8 cup OLIVE OIL
2 tsp. CURRY POWDER
1/2 tsp. GARLIC POWDER
1/4 tsp. ONION POWDER
1/8 tsp. CAYENNE PEPPER
1 cup ALMONDS

Mix all ingredients except almonds and heat in saucepan. Add almonds and stir until coated. Bake the nuts on a foil covered cookie sheet at 300 degrees for about 10 minutes until lightly browned. Stir twice while baking.

Serves 4 - 6, and keeps up to two weeks.

Herb Vegetable Dip

1 pkg. (8 OZ.) CREAM CHEESE, softened
1/4 cup MAYONNAISE
1/4 cup EVAPORATED MILK
2 Tbsp. ONIONS, diced
1 Tbsp. PARSLEY FLAKES
1 tsp. DILL WEED
1 tsp. GARLIC POWDER
TABASCO® to taste

In small bowl, combine all ingredients. Beat until smooth and creamy. Refrigerate 1 to 2 hours or until well chilled. Serve with fresh vegetables.

Yield: 1 2/3 cup

Holiday Nachos

1 lb. lean GROUND BEEF
1 pkg. TACO MIX
1 can REFRIED BEANS
TORTILLA CHIPS
1 sm. can sliced JALAPEÑO PEPPERS
8 oz. MONTEREY JACK CHEESE, shredded

Brown meat in frying pan. Drain fat. Add taco mix, preparing according to package directions. Meanwhile, heat refried beans. Spread layer of tortilla chips in center of an ovenproof platter (a cookie sheet or pizza pan will do). Spoon refried beans evenly over the chips. Put a layer of meat over beans. Add jalapeño peppers as desired. Cover top with cheese. Heat in 375 degree oven for 20 to 25 minutes or until cheese starts to brown. Garnish with chopped **tomatoes** and **green onions** for added holiday color.

Bruschetta

Several cloves GARLIC, peeled
1 loaf FRENCH or ITALIAN BREAD, cut into 1/2-inch
thick slices
OLIVE OIL
SALT and PEPPER to taste
Canned or fresh TOMATOES, diced
Fresh BASIL, coarsely chopped (optional)

Cut garlic cloves in half and rub on bread slices. Discard cloves. Brush olive oil on bread and broil until lightly browned. Season with salt and pepper. Add diced tomatoes to bread and top with basil, if desired.

Spinach Balls

"Everyone compliments these appetizers. They are festive looking, freeze well and are good hot or cold." Jan Catlow, Winter Park.

2 pkg. FROZEN CHOPPED SPINACH, cooked and drained
2 med. ONIONS, chopped
6 EGGS, beaten
1 tsp. GARLIC SALT
3/4 cups BUTTER, melted
2 cups HERB STUFFING MIX
1 cup PARMESAN CHEESE

Mix all ingredients together. Shape into balls about the size of a heaping teaspoon. Place on cookie sheets or other flat pans lined with foil. Bake at 350 degrees for 20 minutes. You may question whether they are really done—they are! Yield: about 45 balls.

CHAPTER THREE

Christmas in the Rockies

Legend has it that when the early Colorado prospectors tired of panning for gold, they strapped skis to their feet and Colorado's ski industry was born. Thus what were once booming mining towns were soon booming with another industry—skiing.

Now famous for its world class skiing, the small town of Telluride still evokes the gold rush era. Some say the town was named after tellurium, a gold-bearing ore, but according to the more poetic version the name is derived from "To Hell You Ride," a reference to the town's rowdy mining history. Like most of Colorado's mining towns, Telluride's prosperity was guided by the ebb and flow of the mining industry. By the time of the Great Depression, the town's population was only 500, a mere fraction of its population during the heyday of the gold rush.

Despite the passage of time, Telluride's Victorian quaintness is very much in evidence, especially during the Christmas season when the mountains glisten with snow and the shop windows twinkle with lights. At Christmas time residents and visitors can experience a Victorian Christmas at the Telluride Museum, participate in the Christmas Eve Torchlight Parade, and join the festivities at the Fireman's Christmas Tree Lighting on Main Street.

Steamboat Springs is another mountain town known for its skiing and colorful past. Mining played a bit part in the area's past, but Steamboat Springs was, and is, a ranching community. Along with the prospectors of old, cowboys left their mark on the state, and indeed on the American psyche in general. Up at dawn, braving cold winter storms, the cowboy toiled long and hard, becoming a symbol of self-reliance and hard work. A ranch town to this day, residents of Steamboat Springs take pride in the town's authenticity and believe that few places can rival the beauty and ambience of their town.

Steamboat Springs has been a haven for skiers since the arrival of Carl Howelson, a champion ski jumper known as "the Flying Norseman", in 1914. Howelsen built a ski jump on the hill that now bears his name and awed the locals with his talents. He also founded the Winter Carnival that continues to this day. True to the spirit of the town, the Winter Carnival Parade features the Steamboat Springs High School Marching Band — on skis.

At Christmas time, Howelson Hill is the site of the annual Christmas Town Party. Other holiday festivities in Steamboat Springs include Christmas in the Rockies Holiday Market, the Mountain Madrigal Singers, the Ski Ball and the Torchlight Parade on New Year's Eve.

Brunch & Breads

Rocky Mountain Style Pancakes with Pear Butter

"I think breakfast is overlooked during the Holidays. It's a good way to get the clan together before a day of skiing. This is a hearty breakfast for us Rocky Mountain types who need energy to ski and shovel snow!" Janet Webb, Steamboat Springs

Pancakes

1 cup CORNMEAL
1 cup WHOLE WHEAT FLOUR
1 tsp. BAKING SODA
1/2 tsp. BAKING POWDER

1/2 tsp. BROWN SUGAR
3 Tbsp. HONEY
2 cups MILK
1 EGG

Pear Butter

2 PEARS, peeled, cored, and chopped into 1/4 inch pieces
1/4 cup WATER
1/2 tsp. CINNAMON
1 Tbsp. SALT

Combine dry ingredients in large bowl. Mix honey, milk and egg with mixer, then add to dry ingredients. While the batter sets to soften the cornmeal, peel and chop the pears. Place in medium saucepan, add water, cinnamon and brown sugar. Bring to a boil, reduce heat, and simmer for 15 minutes until liquid is absorbed. To cook pancakes, lightly oil pan, pour 1/4 cup portions into pan, fry until golden brown. Serve with the pear butter in individual bowls.

Serves 4.

Aunt Rose's Sour Cream Coffee Cake

During the holidays, Jane Yerkman of Blackhawk often makes this family favorite.

1 cup SUGAR
1/4 lb. BUTTER or MARGARINE
1 cup SOUR CREAM
2 EGGS
1 tsp. VANILLA
1 1/2 cups sifted FLOUR
1 1/2 tsp. BAKING POWDER
1 tsp. SODA

Walnut Topping

3/4 cup SUGAR
1 tsp. CINNAMON
1/4 cup WALNUTS

Cream together sugar and butter. Add sour cream and mix — then add eggs and vanilla and mix again. Sift together flour, baking powder and salt; add to mixture. Grease bottom and sides (or spray with cooking spray) of a fluted or spring-release cake pan. Pour in mixture, top with topping and bake at 350 degrees for 30 to 35 minutes. Let cool before removing from pan.

Colorado Heavenly Eggs

Jean Stillwell of Colorado Springs offers two versions of this delectable egg dish. Version 1 is for those watching their fat and cholesterol intake. Jean writes, "This recipe is usually made after a long day of food preparation and served the next morning to give the cook a nice break at the beginning of the day. The fruit enhances the flavors, and the sour cream and/or picante sauce gives it that Southwest flavor."

Version 1:

2 to 3 packages of EGGBEATERS®
1/2 cup CONDENSED CANNED MILK
2 cups SKIMMED MILK
5-6 slices of DRY DAY-OLD BREAD
1/2 cup each of a variety of VEGETABLES

Version 2:

4 to 6 EGGS, well beaten
1/2 cup CREAM or BUTTERMILK
2 cups WHOLE MILK
1/2 loaf of DAY-OLD FRENCH or ITALIAN BREAD
1/2 cup each of a variety of VEGETABLES
1/2 cup CHEESE and/or MEAT, cut into bite size pieces

Spray cooking spray or spread butter on a 9 x 13 x 2 pan. Spread bread broken into small bite size pieces over pan. Cover bread with mushrooms, onions, tomatoes, celery or any combination of fresh or leftover vegetables. Add meat or cheese if desired. Mix eggs well, add condensed milk or cream, continue to beat, adding milk a cup at a time until all is frothy. Pour egg/milk mixture over dry ingredients. Cover and refrigerate until the next morning.

Preheat oven to 350 degrees (375 degrees in high elevations), and bake uncovered for 1 1/2 hours until golden brown. Slice into chunks, like a dish cake, and serve with sliced fruit, sour cream and picante sauce on the side.

Serves 4 - 6.

Zucchini Squash Marmalade

A colorful marmalade for holiday breakfast toast or rolls.

5 cups ZUCCHINI SQUASH, shredded
1 can (20 oz.) CRUSHED PINEAPPLE and JUICE
3/4 cup LEMON JUICE
3/4 cup ORANGE JUICE
4 cups SUGAR
1/4 cup MARASCHINO CHERRIES
1 package (3 oz.) ORANGE JELLO®

Wash and peel squash (about 5 inches long in size). Shred 5 cups squash, add one 20-ounce can crushed pineapple with juice, and then the lemon and orange juices and the sugar. Mix in a large bowl and let set overnight. Next day, add the maraschino cherries and cook about 35 minutes, stirring frequently to prevent burning. When mixture begins to thicken, add the orange Jello and stir until dissolved. Spoon into scalded jelly jars and cover with paraffin.

Yield: 6 pints

The Holden House

Holden House was built in 1902 by Isabel Holden, the widow of former rancher and prosperous Colorado Springs businessman Daniel M. Holden. The Holdens had six children and although Daniel Holden died in 1896 of cholera, Isabel was 85 years old at her death in 1931. The memories of Isabel and her children live on today at Holden House 1902 Bed and Breakfast Inn, which was restored in 1986 by its current owners and innkeepers Sallie and Welling Clark. The following five recipes are some of Sallie's holiday favorites.

Southwestern Eggs Fiesta

This festive looking dish adds a touch of red and green to the breakfast table.

6 INDIVIDUAL SOUFFLÉ DISHES (5-8 oz. size)
12 EGGS
3 snack size FLOUR TORTILLAS
6 oz. CHEDDAR CHEESE SLICES
BACON BITS or CRUMBLED COOKED TURKEY BACON
SOUR CREAM for topping
Mild PICANTE SAUCE for topping
PARSLEY for garnish
CILANTRO

Grease the soufflé dishes well with non-stick spray and break two eggs into each dish. Slice tortillas in half and place in dishes with flat edge down and outside eggs to form a U-shape around outer edge of dish. Top with 1 ounce slice of cheddar cheese and crumbled bacon or bacon bits and sprinkle with a dash of cilantro. Bake at 375 degrees for 30 minutes or until eggs are done, cheese is melted and tortilla is slightly brown. Top with a dab of sour cream and one teaspoon of picante sauce. Sprinkle a dash of cilantro on top and serve on a plate. Parsley is optional.

Baked Islander French Toast

Holden House

An exceptionally good treat for Christmas morning.

1 cup BROWN SUGAR
1/2 cup BUTTER
2 Tbsp. CORN SYRUP
1/2 cup FLAKED COCONUT
1/2 cup SLIVERED ALMONDS
2 medium BANANAS, sliced
6 EGGS
1 1/2 cups MILK
1/2 tsp. PINEAPPLE FLAVORING
1/2 tsp. COCONUT FLAVORING
1/2 tsp. BANANA FLAVORING
9 slices POTATO BREAD
Dash NUTMEG for garnish
6 rings of CANNED PINEAPPLE
WHIPPED CREAM

The night before, melt brown sugar, butter and corn syrup in microwave. Grease 9 x 13 pan and pour melted sugar mixture in bottom of baking pan. Sprinkle flaked coconut and slivered almonds on top and lay banana slices over sugar mixture. Whip eggs, milk, and flavorings. Slice bread crosswise and place in dish over sugar mixture. Pour egg mixture over slices of bread. Leave in refrigerator overnight. Bake at 400 degrees for 20 to 30 minutes. When serving, turn over and place on plates with sugar/coconut/banana/almond mixture on top. Serve 3 slices to each person and top with a dollop of whipped cream. Garnish with a ring of pineapple and a sprinkle of coconut and fresh ground nutmeg.

Serves 6, but can easily be adapted for more.

Carob Chip Muffins

Holden House

These muffins are exceptionally good for an afternoon Christmas tea as well as holiday breakfasts.

1 EGG, slightly beaten
1/3 cup MARGARINE or BUTTER, softened
1/2 cup MILK
1/2 cup SOUR CREAM
2 1/2 cups FLOUR
1 Tbsp. BAKING POWDER
1/3 cup SUGAR
1/3 cup BROWN SUGAR
1/2 tsp. each CINNAMON, NUTMEG AND GINGER
Pinch SALT
1 cup CAROB CHIPS
1/2 cup CHOPPED WALNUTS FOR TOPPING
SUGAR, for sprinkling on top

Cream together egg, butter, milk and sour cream. In separate bowl, combine flour, baking powder, sugars, spices and salt. Add dry mixture to egg mixture. When completely mixed, add carob chips. Evenly divide mixture into a well greased 12-muffin tin. Top with chopped walnuts and sprinkle a little sugar over the top of muffins and bake in a preheated 400-degree oven for 25 to 30 minutes or until done and lightly browned.

Italiano Eggs Florentine

Holden House

This Italian dish fills the house with nutmeg scents. It can be used for breakfast or as a pre-holiday dinner entree.

2 PILLSBURY® ALL READY CRUSTS
Eight 12 ounce size Quiche Dishes
4 EGGS
2 cups MILK
4 Tbsp. FLOUR
1 pkg. (16 ounce) FROZEN SPINACH
1 cup shredded SWISS, JACK or MOZZARELLA CHEESE
8 slices TURKEY BACON, sliced in half
ITALIAN SEASONING
GROUND NUTMEG
1 sm. jar of MARINARA SAUCE
SHREDDED PARMESAN CHEESE, for garnish
FRESH PARSLEY

Divide each pie crust into four sections and place in quiche dish (will form a triangular-shaped crust). Beat eggs, milk and flour together and set aside. Evenly divide thawed spinach and place into bottom of each quiche dish on top of crust. Pour egg and milk mixture over spinach, top with shredded cheese, lay 2 half slices of bacon over cheese, and sprinkle with a dash of Italian seasoning and dash of nutmeg. Bake in a 375-degree oven for 30 to 40 minutes or until quiche is firm and slightly brown on top. Remove from oven and garnish with 3 tablespoons of marinara sauce, a sprinkle of parmesan cheese and a sprig of fresh parsley. Serves 8.

German Puff Pancakes with Spiced Apples

Holden House

1 cup MILK
1 cup FLOUR
6 EGGS
2 tsp. VANILLA
8 pats of BUTTER or MARGARINE
5 med. APPLES, any variety
1/2 cup BROWN SUGAR
1/2 tsp. each CINNAMON, NUTMEG and GINGER
1/2 cup MINCEMEAT
4 Tbsp. BUTTER or MARGARINE
GROUND NUTMEG, for garnish
WHIPPED TOPPING, for garnish
8 SLICED APPLE WEDGES, for garnish

Whip milk, flour, eggs and vanilla. Set aside. Place pat of butter in each bowl. Preheat bowls in 400-degree oven for 10 to 15 minutes or until butter is popping hot. In the meantime, cut apples into chunks and place in frying pan with butter. Cook for 15 minutes or until apples are moderately soft. Add a bit of water if apples become too dry while cooking. When cooked, add cinnamon, nutmeg, ginger, brown sugar and mincemeat to apples. Continue cooking another 5 to 10 minutes or until well mixed and hot. When butter in dishes is popping hot, add an even measurement of pancake batter to each dish. Turn up oven to 425 degrees for ten minutes, then back down to 400 degrees for another 5 minutes or until pancakes are puffed up and slightly brown on edges. Remove from oven, place an even measure of apples in center of each pancake. Top with dollop of whipped topping and sprinkle with fresh nutmeg. Place a wedge of apple on top as garnish and serve on cloth doilies on plates. Be careful! These are extremely hot and may crack plates if doilies are not used.

Denver Frittata

1/3 cup BUTTER or MARGARINE
1/2 cup fresh MUSHROOMS, sliced
1/2 cup GREEN and RED PEPPERS, chopped
1/4 cup ONION, finely chopped
6 EGGS
2 Tbsp. WATER
1 cup COOKED HAM, chopped
1 cup grated CHEDDAR CHEESE

Melt butter in a 10-inch skillet. Add mushrooms, peppers and onion. Cook over medium heat until tender, about 3 or 4 minutes. In medium bowl combine eggs and water, and beat until frothy. Stir in ham and half of the cheese. Pour into skillet. Stir gently over medium heat to cook evenly on bottom, approximately 3 to 4 minutes. As egg mixture sets, lift edges with spatula to allow uncooked egg to flow underneath. Cover and continue cooking until eggs are set, another 3 to 4 minutes. Sprinkle with the remaining cheese and cut into wedges.
Serves 4.

Granny's Banana Bread

Perfect for gift giving or for those unexpected guests.

1 1/2 cup SUGAR (half brown, half white)
1 cup SHORTENING (oil can be substituted)
3 EGGS
4 Tbsp. MAYONNAISE
2 tsp. BAKING SODA, dissolved in water
4 ripe BANANAS, mashed in 3 cups FLOUR

Cream sugar and shortening. Mix in eggs and mayonnaise. Add baking soda in water. Add bananas in flour. Pour into loaf pan. Bake at 350 degrees for approximately 45 minutes. Cover with foil after 30 minutes if top is getting too brown.

Spinach-Mushroom Quiche

The Queen Anne Bed & Breakfast Inn

Custard:
 5 lg. EGGS
 1 1/2 cups HEAVY CREAM
 Pinch SALT
 Pinch WHITE PEPPER
 1/8 tsp. NUTMEG
 1/4 tsp. PAPRIKA

Filling:
 8 oz. FROZEN SPINACH
 1 sm. can SLICED or CHOPPED MUSHROOMS

Blend custard ingredients. Thaw spinach and let drain. Squeeze out as much moisture as possible. Place spinach on bottom of pie shell. Drain mushrooms and spread a layer over the spinach. Pour custard over all, filling shell to the top edge. Preheat oven 350 degrees and bake 20 to 22 minutes or until the filling is no longer liquid and is well set.

Serves 6.

Note: Freeze immediately if not to be served at once. To thaw, place in the refrigerator the day before (it takes more than a night), or can be thawed in the microwave. Because of the egg content, do not thaw by setting out on kitchen counters.

The Queen Anne Bed & Breakfast Inn

The Queen Anne Bed & Breakfast Inn faces Benedict Fountain Park in the Clement Historic District of Downtown Denver. The Inn consists of two National Trust Registry Victorian Homes. At Christmas time, innkeeper Tom King carries on an old family tradition by placing a freshly cut Christmas tree adorned with white lights in every guest room. A 10-foot fir graces the living room.

Lemony Orange Muffins

The Queen Anne Bed & Breakfast Inn

1 cup SUGAR
2/3 cup SHORTENING
2 EGGS
2 Tbsp. freshly squeezed LEMON JUICE
3 cups sifted all purpose FLOUR
3 tsp. BAKING POWDER
1/2 tsp. SALT
1 tsp. GROUND NUTMEG
1 cup MILK

Orange Glaze

1 1/2 cups POWDERED SUGAR
4 Tbsp. freshly squeezed ORANGE JUICE
2 Tbsp. grated ORANGE ZEST

Orange Butter

3 Tbsp. POWDERED SUGAR
2 Tbsp. grated ORANGE ZEST
1/2 cup softened UNSALTED BUTTER

Cream sugar, shortening, eggs, and lemon juice. Sift together flour, baking powder, salt, and nutmeg; add to creamed mixture alternately with milk, beating well after each addition. Pour into 24 greased or paper-lined muffin cups 2/3 full and bake at 350 degrees for 20 to 25 minutes. Brush muffins with orange glaze while still warm and serve with chilled orange butter.

Victorian Holiday Brunch

According to Tom King, Innkeeper of The Queen Anne B & B, "well-to-do Victorians had a substantial breakfast at perhaps 10 AM. It was originally served almost as a 'help yourself' choice with the serving dishes on the table in every available space. Later, particularly in this country, breakfast became 'serve yourself' from a buffet display. However, the buffet presentation still followed the approach of wide variety. The table featured elaborate plants and flower displays, such as roses and trailing ivy, and a wrapped gift at each place."

Christmas Bread

A great bread for holiday gift-giving!

2 cups sifted FLOUR
4 tsp. BAKING POWDER
Scant 3/4 cup SUGAR
1/4 tsp. SALT
1 cup CANDIED MIXED FRUITS, chopped
1 cup NUTS, chopped
2 EGGS
1 cup MILK
3 Tbsp. BUTTER, melted

Sift flour, baking powder, sugar and salt. Add fruit and nuts. Beat eggs and combine with milk and melted shortening. Add to flour mixture, stirring just enough to moisten the flour. Pour into well-greased loaf pan and let stand 30 minutes. Bake 1 hour at 375 degrees.

Potica

*It wouldn't be Christmas in Pueblo without Potica
(pronounced po-TEET-sa).*

1/2 cup warm WATER
3 pkgs. DRY YEAST
3 EGGS, well beaten
3/4 cup BUTTER
1 pt. scalded MILK, cooled to warm
3/4 cup SUGAR
1 1/2 tsp. SALT
8 to 10 cups FLOUR

Dissolve the dry yeast in 1/2 cup warm water. Beat eggs and add to the yeast mixture. Add the butter and the pint of cooled milk. Mix sugar and salt, and add. Add flour gradually. Knead dough about 10 minutes. Let rise in a warm place about one hour.

Filling:

2 lbs. of NUT MEATS, ground with a meat grinder
2 cups SUGAR
3/4 cup HONEY
1 13-oz can CONDENSED MILK
1 tsp. CINNAMON
3/4 cup BUTTER
3 EGGS, well beaten

Glaze:

1 EGG, beaten

Mix all the filling ingredients and warm. When dough has risen, dump dough on large table covered with lightly floured sheet. Roll dough some; then pull until thin (easier to pull with two people). Spread filling on dough and roll. Place dough in greased and floured bread pans. Brush glaze over all the dough. Let rise one-half hour in warm place. Bake one hour at 350 degrees.

Yield: 5 loaves

CHAPTER FOUR

A Frontier Christmas

A frontier Christmas is recreated every year at Bent's Fort, a restored trading post from the era of the mountain men and fur trapper. The trading post was established by four brothers, Charles, William, Robert and George Bent, and their business partner, Ceran St. Vrain, and was one of the most successful trading posts of the old West, operating for about 16 years. The partners had a good head for business and operated other trading posts throughout the West, though none were quite as large or as successful as Bent's Fort.

Buffalo was the staple of trade for the trading post. Indians brought in buffalo robes (up to 10,000 per year) as well as meat and leather. But Bent's Fort also traded with fur trappers for beaver pelts. Back in the civilized cities of New York and Paris, beaver felt hats were all the rage, but the dictates of fashion and the advent of silk hats made beavers a less reliable source of income.

Visitors to Bent's Fort today will be greeted by folks dressed in buckskin, and at Christmas time Bent's Fort recreates a Frontier Christmas, circa 1840-1850. As part of its living history program, the Fort presents a mingling of American colonial customs with Mexican traditions, featuring such things as a pinata; a yule log; Las Posadas, a recreation of Joseph and Mary's search for lodging; and Los Abuelos, in which grandparents dress up and scare the youngsters before presenting them with a treat of some sort. Visitors also witness the arrival of a wagon from Missouri bearing goodies and letters that will be read aloud on the village square. Plum pudding and gingerbread cookies are also served.

Salads

Taffy Apple Salad

This salad is easy to make and is great for a holiday buffet. Kids love it!

1 can PINEAPPLE CHUNKS and JUICE
2 cups SUGAR
1 EGG, beaten
1 1/2 tsp. VINEGAR
1 Tbsp. FLOUR
2 - 3 lg. APPLES, diced
1 sm. can PEANUTS
2 cups MINI-MARSHMALLOWS
1 container (8 oz.) WHIPPED TOPPING

Combine pineapple juice, sugar, egg, vinegar and flour; heat until thickened. Cool. In a large bowl, combine sauce with remaining ingredients.

Christmas Jello

This colorful salad can be made up ahead of time and makes a colorful addition to a holiday dinner or lunch.

1 pkg. GREEN JELLO® (lime)
1 can (20 oz.) CRUSHED PINEAPPLE, drained
1 container (8 oz.) WHIPPED TOPPING
1 pkg. (3 oz.) CREAM CHEESE
1 pkg. RED JELLO® (strawberry or raspberry)

Mix green Jello using ice method on package. Drain crushed pineapple and add. Put into mold and let set. Mix the whipped topping and cream cheese. Add on top of green Jello. Mix red Jello, again using ice method. Pour over the filling. Refrigerate.

Serves 10-12.

Pasta Salad

Serve with a loaf of crusty French bread at a Christmas luncheon as an alternative to heavy and rich foods.

1 pkg. (12 oz.) rainbow ROTELLE (or other curly pasta)
1 sm. ZUCCHINI, sliced and cut into half moons
1 sm. YELLOW SQUASH, sliced and cut into half moons
1 sm. bunch BROCCOLI, cut into small flowerets
1/2 cup CHEDDAR CHEESE, diced
1/2 cup PEPPER JACK CHEESE
1/2 pkg. (about 1-2 oz.) SLICED SALAMI
1 Tbsp. dried PARSLEY
BOTTLED ITALIAN DRESSING
PARMESAN CHEESE
SALT
Freshly ground BLACK PEPPER

Prepare pasta according to package directions. Meanwhile, steam vegetables until tender crisp. In a large bowl, combine all ingredients except salad dressing and Parmesan cheese. Pour desired amount of dressing over all and liberally sprinkle with Parmesan cheese. Salt and pepper to taste.

Zesty Bean Salad

1 can (15 oz.) GARBANZO BEANS, drained
1/4 cup BOTTLED VINAIGRETTE SALAD DRESSING
1/4 cup fresh PARSLEY, chopped
2 Tbsp. CHILI SAUCE
1/2 tsp. OREGANO LEAVES
CRISP SALAD GREENS

Combine all ingredients except salad greens; chill thoroughly. Serve on salad greens.

Serves 3 - 4.

Christmas Bean Salad

This is a very pretty salad at Christmas time, with the greens and the reds. It also keeps very well in the refrigerator for up to two weeks, so you can make it ahead of time

1 can French-style GREEN BEANS
1 sm. can LESEUR® PEAS
1/4 cup CELERY, chopped
1/4 cup GREEN PEPPER, chopped
1/4 cup ONION, chopped
1 sm. jar PIMENTOS, chopped

Mix in medium sized bowl and set aside.

Dressing:
1 tsp. SALT
1/4 cup VEGETABLE OIL
1 cup SUGAR
1/2 cup VINEGAR

Mix well and pour over vegetables. Let set overnight refrigerated, stirring 2 or 3 times. Drain well before serving. Serves 8 - 10.

Potato Herb Salad

6 - 7 med. POTATOES
1/4 cup ONION, finely chopped
2 Tbsp. SHALLOTS, finely chopped
1 clove GARLIC, finely chopped
1/4 cup fresh PARSLEY, chopped
1 - 2 tsp. HOT GREEN CHILES, chopped
1/2 tsp. TARRAGON
1/2 cup dry WHITE WINE
1/4 cup OLIVE OIL
2 Tbsp. RED WINE VINEGAR
Freshly ground BLACK PEPPER
SALT

Place potatoes in large saucepan and cover with cold water. Bring to a boil and simmer until tender, approximately 20 minutes. Peel potatoes when they are just cool enough to handle. Cut potatoes into slices. Put potatoes in a bowl and add remaining ingredients. Gently stir.

Serves 8-10.

CHAPTER FIVE

Christmas in Georgetown

Once a booming mining town, Georgetown is today known for its Christmas Market. An annual event since the late 1950s, the market is reminiscent of the Swedish Julmarkand and German Christmarket celebrations held in European mountain towns.

The Market runs for two weekends early in December and features handmade crafts and homebaked foods. Festivities include horse-drawn hayrides, Christmas carolers, dancers, and bagpipers. The highlights of the market are the appearance of St. Nicholas and the Santa Lucia Procession.

Georgetown's St. Nick was inspired by celebrations of the Feast of St. Nicholas in Holland, Germany and Austria. According to legend, St. Nicholas was a fourth century bishop. Astride his white steed, he rode through the streets asking children whether they had been bad or good. The good ones received sweets, while the bad ones earned a switch. In the United States today the feast of St. Nicholas has become one of the highlights of the Christmas season for many families. On the eve of December 6, children leave their shoes out before they go to bed and the next morning —if they've been good—they will find their shoes filled with candy, fruit, or perhaps a small toy.

The celebrations surrounding Santa Lucia originated in Sweden as a tribute to Saint Lucia, a fourth century martyr who brought food to her fellow Christians in the catacombs. On the morning of December 13, the oldest girl in the family dons a white robe, red sash, and a crown of twigs with nine lighted candles. Awakening the rest of the family, she brings them sweet buns (called Lucia buns) and coffee or a sweet drink and sings a special song. When everyone is dressed, the family has breakfast by candlelight. Like many towns in Sweden, the Georgetown Christmas Market features a Santa Lucia Processional concluding with a performance by a children's choir.

Main Dishes

Christmas Chowder

According to John Wheats of Telluride, a flamboyant 80-year-old woman whispered this recipe into his one good ear before they skied The Plunge in Telluride. He states that, on a cold, chilly evening, this chowder will not only fill the gullet, but will calm your nerves and improve your love life.

**SCALLOPS, WHOLE CLAMS, SHRIMP, CRAB,
SOLE, or GOOD QUALITY SEAFOOD**
10 ozs. WHITE WINE
2 med. ONIONS, chopped
6-8 med. POTATOES, diced
6-8 cloves GARLIC, chopped
1 tsp. SALT
1 tsp. GINGER
1/2 stick BUTTER
1 pt. HEAVY CREAM
1/2 gal. WHOLE MILK
1/2 tsp. WHITE or BLACK PEPPER
Pinch of ITALIAN SEASONING
1/2 lb. fresh SIDE PORK

Marinate all seafood in wine for two hours. Boil onions and potatoes in salt water; drain. Put seafood and wine with onions and potatoes in a large pot and add chopped garlic, ginger, butter, heavy cream, milk, pepper, and Italian seasoning. Heat slowly. **Never boil or scald**. Fry side pork and add last to top of chowder. If chunky or thick, add more milk to taste. This dish will last for a week in the refrigerator; the longer it sits, the better the flavor.

Serves 8-10.

Some Like It Hot Chicken Timbales

After a long day of Christmas shopping, "this is a good recipe because it is quick and easy to make. You can eat the timbales hot or cold, and you can add any sauce or salsa or "whatever" over the top or eat as is. It is easily accompanied by either fruit or vegetable salad." Janice E. James, Kirk

2 cups diced, cooked CHICKEN or two 6-ounce cans of chicken
1 cup soft BREAD CRUMBS or any flavor dry STUFFING MIX
1/4 cup ONION, finely chopped
2 Tbsp. GREEN CHILES, chopped (or hotter peppers to taste)
3 Tbsp. melted BUTTER OR MARGARINE
1/2 tsp. CRUSHED RED PEPPER
1/2 tsp. SALT
1 cup EVAPORATED MILK
2 EGGS
1/4 cup grated extra sharp CHEDDAR CHEESE

Combine all ingredients and mix well. Place in six muffin cups which have been sprayed with cooking spray or greased with other shortening. Bake in moderate oven, 350 degrees, for 35 to 40 minutes. Remove and serve.

Serves 6.

Roast Turkey with Stuffing & Gravy

Even though Thanksgiving and turkey with all the trimmings was only a month before, many people can't imagine Christmas dinner without a succulent roast turkey.

Turkey

1 TURKEY
BUTTER or MARGARINE
SALT
PEPPER

Remove giblets and reserve for gravy. Rinse turkey with cold water. Stuff the body and neck cavities before trussing. Rub butter or margarine all over turkey. Sprinkle with salt and pepper. Place breast side down on rack in roasting pan. Roast in 325 degree oven, allowing 12 minutes per pound. Baste with melted butter every 20 to 30 minutes. Turn turkey over after 1 1/2 hours. Turkey is done when meat thermometer registers 170 degrees in breast meat, 185 degrees in thigh meat. Remove to platter and make gravy.

Stuffing

Plain or fancy? Outside the bird or in? Or maybe you call it dressing. Whatever form it takes, stuffing is an absolute must with turkey. Here's a good basic recipe. For a more elaborate one, see the recipe for Oyster Stuffing in the chapter on side dishes.

3 qts. BREAD CUBES (homemade or packaged
**   or a combination of both)**
1/2 lb. BUTTER or MARGARINE
1 lg. ONION, finely chopped
6 - 8 stalks CELERY, chopped

(Continued on next page)

1/2 cup PARSLEY, chopped
1 Tbsp. THYME
1 Tbsp. SAGE
1 1/2 tsp. MARJORAM
1 tsp. BLACK PEPPER, freshly ground
SALT to taste

Melt about 4 tablespoons butter in a large frying pan. Sauté onions and celery until soft. Place bread crumbs and seasonings in a large bowl. Melt the rest of the butter and add it, along with cooked onions and celery, to the bread crumbs. Mix lightly until bread is coated. If you prefer a moister stuffing, add additional melted butter, water or chicken or turkey stock. Don't overstuff the bird, as the stuffing expands as it cooks.

Yield: about 9 cups (enough for a small turkey).

Gravy

GIBLETS
1 ONION, chopped
2 - 3 stalks, CELERY, chopped
4 - 5 Tbsp. FAT FROM TURKEY DRIPPINGS
3 - 4 Tbsp. FLOUR
SALT
PEPPER

While turkey is cooking, boil giblets in 3 to 4 cups water along with onion and celery. When turkey is done, remove from roasting pan. Skim off most of the fat, leaving about 4 tablespoons. Scrape the bottom of the pan to loosen the brown drippings. Make a paste out of the flour and a small amount of giblet water. Add to pan drippings. Stir constantly over medium high heat until lightly browned. Add giblet water gradually, stirring constantly until smooth. Add salt and pepper to taste. Bring to a boil and simmer 15 - 20 minutes.

Quick & Easy Hamburger Soup

1 1/2 pounds HAMBURGER
1 lg. ONION, chopped fine or diced
1 tsp. GARLIC POWDER or 1 clove GARLIC, mashed
1 BAY LEAF
1 tsp. THYME LEAVES
1 tsp. ROSEMARY
1 tsp. SWEET BASIL
SALT and PEPPER to taste
2 cubes BEEF BOUILLON
1 can TOMATO SAUCE
1 can DICED TOMATOES
3 POTATOES, diced
2 CARROTS, sliced thinly
1 rib CELERY, cut in fine pieces
1 TURNIP or PARSNIP, diced
1 can NAVY BEANS
1/2 head small CABBAGE, red or green, shredded thinly
WATER as needed
TABASCO® SAUCE to taste

Brown hamburger in a skillet or pan. Pour off any excess fat/grease. In a large kettle or stew pot, put the hamburger, onion, garlic, bay leaf, thyme, rosemary, basil, salt and pepper, tomato sauce and water to make soup the consistency you like. Cook about thirty minutes. Add all other ingredients, plus more water if it is needed. Stir all to blend. Simmer until vegetables are done, and the soup is desired consistency. (Remove bay leaf before serving.)

Winter Picnic Chili

Excellent for picnics! Cook beforehand and transport in a cast iron dutch oven or kettle. Heat up over campfire until it comes to a boil.

1 lb. lean BEEF OR TURKEY, ground	1/2 tsp. SALT
1 med. ONION, chopped	1/2 tsp. BLACK PEPPER
1 clove GARLIC, chopped	1 1/2 tsp. CHILI POWDER
2 cans STEWED TOMATOES, chopped	WATER, as needed to thin

Brown ground meat with onions and garlic. Drain well. Add tomatoes and seasonings and simmer for 1 to 2 hours, adding water as necessary to thin.

Turkey Casserole

A creative way to use up that leftover Christmas turkey.

2 EGGS, well beaten
2 slices ONION, chopped
4 stalks CELERY, chopped
4 sprigs PARSLEY, minced
1 1/2 cups BREAD STUFFING
3 cups TURKEY, cooked, chopped
1 can CREAM OF MUSHROOM SOUP
1 CHICKEN BOUILLON CUBE, dissolved in 1 cup water
1/2 cup MILK
POTATO CHIPS

Mix together well-beaten eggs, onion, celery, parsley, bread stuffing and turkey. Mix cream of mushroom soup with the dissolved bouillon cube and add milk. Mix all together and pour into a 2-quart casserole dish. Cover with crushed potato chips and bake at 325 degrees for 60 minutes.

Makes 6 servings.

Wild Rice Casserole

1 cup WILD RICE
5 cups WATER
1 tsp. SALT
1 pound GROUND BEEF
2 cups sliced CARROT COINS
1 large chopped ONION
2 cups chopped CELERY
1 can (4 oz.) MUSHROOMS
2 cans (10-3/4 oz. ea.) CREAM OF MUSHROOM SOUP
4 cups WATER

Cook wild rice in a heavy saucepan in five cups of water until kernels are open and tender, but not mushy (about 45 minutes). Brown ground meat, mix with wild rice. In two 2-quart greased casseroles, layer, starting with the wild rice and meat mixture, then vegetables and mushroom and end with the rice/meat mixture.

Heat the cream of mushroom soup and water. Pour over the contents of casseroles until it covers the mixture. Bake at 350 degrees for 60-70 minutes.

If desired, biscuits can be added to the top after one hour. Return to oven and cook an additional 10-15 minutes until biscuits are done.

Serves 10-12 people.

Lasagna

After Christmas Eve services, it's a tradition in many families to come home to a delicious dinner of lasagna. You can prepare it ahead of time and refrigerate, but be sure to increase the cooking time.

1 med. ONION
2 cloves GARLIC, chopped
4 Tbsp. OLIVE OIL
1 lb. GROUND CHUCK
1/2 lb. ITALIAN SAUSAGE
1 can (28 oz.) TOMATOES
2 cans (6 oz.ea.) TOMATO PASTE
1/2 cup WATER
1 tsp. SALT
1/2 tsp. BASIL LEAVES
1/2 tsp. OREGANO LEAVES
1/8 tsp. CRUSHED RED PEPPER
2 EGGS
1 1/2 lb. RICOTTA CHEESE
1/4 cup PARSLEY, chopped
1 lb. LASAGNA NOODLES
1 LB. MOZZARELLA CHEESE, sliced
PARMESAN CHEESE, freshly grated

Sauté onions and garlic in olive oil. Remove from pan. Brown meat and drain fat. Return onions and garlic to pan and add tomatoes, tomato paste, water and seasonings. Simmer. Meanwhile, mix eggs with ricotta cheese and chopped parsley. Cook lasagna until soft but firm. Layer noodles, sauce, ricotta mixture, mozzarella and parmesan in a 13 x 9 pan. Bake at 375 degrees for 25 minutes, or until warm and bubbly.

Chicken Enchiladas

Great for an informal holiday gathering.

4 - 5 CHICKEN BREASTS, boiled and chopped
1 pkg. (8 oz.) CREAM CHEESE
8 oz. MONTEREY JACK CHEESE WITH JALAPEÑOS, grated
1 EGG
10 - 12 TORTILLAS
1 can (large) ENCHILADA SAUCE
CHEDDAR CHEESE, shredded (optional)
SOUR CREAM
LETTUCE, shredded

Combine cream cheese and jack cheese and heat in saucepan over low heat, stirring continuously until completely melted. Remove from heat and let cool a bit. Add egg and mix until well blended. Add chicken. Heat tortillas in a hot frying pan. Fold chicken mixture into tortillas. Place in 13 x 9 baking pan sprayed with cooking spray. Pour enchilada sauce over the top and bake at 350 degrees for 30 minutes or until bubbly. If desired, add shredded cheddar cheese to top during the last five minutes. Remove from oven and top with sour cream and shredded lettuce, if desired.

Christmas Goose with Port Wine Gravy

1 GOOSE, 10 - 12 lbs.
SALT
PEPPER

Remove giblets and reserve for gravy. Rinse goose with cold water. Pat dry, sprinkle with salt and pepper inside and out, and skewer or sew up opening. Pierce the skin all over with fork to release fat while cooking. Place goose, breast side down, on rack in roasting pan. Roast in 325 degree oven for 3 - 4 hours. Bird is done when juices run clear from cut on upper thigh.

Port Wine Gravy

GOOSE GIBLETS
1 ONION, chopped
2 - 3 stalks, CELERY, chopped
1 BAY LEAF
1/2 cup PORT WINE
SALT
PEPPER
1/2 Tbsp. CORNSTARCH

While goose is cooking, boil giblets (except liver) in water with onion, celery and bay leaf. In a medium saucepan, pour 2 to 3 tablespoons of fat from the goose, and add 2 cups water from the boiled giblets. Bring to a boil and add 1/2 cup port. Season with salt and pepper. Thicken with 1/2 tablespoon cornstarch mixed with an equal amount of water. Stir until sauce boils and thickens, about 1 minute.

The following excerpt is from an article in the December 21, 1913 edition of the Rocky Mountain News *offering this recipe for cooking a goose.*

Recipe for Cooking a Goose

by Florence Naylor Doty

There has been a request from one of our patrons for an authentic recipe for cooking a goose, as so many persons have the disastrous result of getting the goose either too dry or too greasy.

. . . There is nothing which can be made to taste better than a properly cooked goose, The goose needs different treatment from any other kind of bird, owing to its very strong flavor.

After it has had all the pin feathers removed and has been duly washed and scrubbed in hot suds, it should be drawn and then thoroughly washed in cold water and whipped. Stuff, truss and season, laying a piece of salt pork over the top, which is held in place by a toothpick.

Place on a rack in a dripping pan (never without the rack) and bake two hours, basting every fifteen minutes with the fat from the bottom of the pan. Remove the fat from the breast and serve with apples which have been filed with apple sauce.

Now comes the best part — the prune stuffing. Honest goose without prune stuffing is like a needle without an eye; the essential part has been left out.

To make the stuffing, the prunes must be soaked overnight, drained in the morning, and covered with boiling water and cooked until nearly tender. Blanch one cup rice, add enough prune juice and water to make three cups in all, and add a teaspoon of salt and cook until the rice is tender. Then add the prunes, which have been chopped, blanched and boiled, and half a cup of butter, a half teaspoon of paprika and a little cinnamon if desired.

After mixing thoroughly it is ready for use.

Shrimp Linguine

1 can (28 oz.) ITALIAN STYLE TOMATOES
1 med. ONION
2 cloves GARLIC, chopped
4 Tbsp. OLIVE OIL
1/2 tsp. SALT
1/2 tsp. BASIL LEAVES
1/2 tsp. OREGANO LEAVES
1 BAY LEAF
1/8 tsp. CRUSHED RED PEPPER
1 can (8 oz.) TOMATO PASTE
1 pkg. (12 oz.) LINGUINE
1 lb. SHRIMP, peeled & deveined

Bring tomatoes to a boil and simmer until reduced by about half. Meanwhile, sauté onions and garlic in olive oil. Add onions and garlic to tomatoes. Add salt, basil, oregano, bay leaf and red pepper. Add about 1/2 can of the tomato paste to thicken. Simmer 30 minutes. Return to a boil when you are ready to cook linguine. As linguine goes into water, add shrimp to sauce. Remove from heat and let sit while linguine cooks.

Serves 4.

Christmas Ham

1/2 HAM, shank end
WHOLE CLOVES
3/4 cup ORANGE JUICE
1/2 cup BROWN SUGAR
1/2 cup WATER
2 tsp. DRY MUSTARD

Score the outside of the ham in a diamond pattern. Place a whole clove in the center of each diamond. Combine orange juice, brown sugar, water and dry mustard for basting sauce. Bake in 325 degree oven for about two hours, basting several times. Ham is done when meat thermometer registers 160 degrees.

Chicken Paprika

*An elegant dish for a holiday dinner with
family and friends.*

2 Tbsp. LARD
3 lbs. FRYING CHICKEN
SALT
1 cup ONIONS, finely chopped
1/2 tsp. GARLIC, finely chopped
1 1/2 Tbsp. PAPRIKA
1 cup CHICKEN STOCK
2 Tbsp. FLOUR
1 1/2 cups SOUR CREAM

Heat lard in a large frying pan. Salt chicken and fry in lard until brown. Remove from pan. Add onions and garlic and cook about 8 minutes. Remove pan from heat and stir in paprika. Return to heat and add chicken stock. Bring to a boil. Return chicken to frying pan and bring to a boil again. Turn heat to low and cover. Simmer 20-30 minutes. Remove chicken. Combine flour and sour cream and add to juices. Simmer 6 to 8 minutes longer. Add chicken and simmer an additional 3 to 4 minutes.

Serves 6-8.

Hot Turkey Casserole

Wondering what to do with all that leftover turkey?

2 cups cooked TURKEY, diced
1 cup MAYONNAISE
1 cup CELERY, diced
2 Tbsp. LEMON JUICE
1 Tbsp. ONION, diced
1/2 cup NUTS, chopped
1/2 tsp. SALT
Dash PEPPER
1/2 cup grated CHEDDAR CHEESE
1 cup crushed POTATO CHIPS

Mix all ingredients except cheese and potato chips. Put into individual casseroles or a 1-quart casserole. Top with cheese and potato chips. Bake in very hot 450 degree oven for 10 minutes or until heated through.

Serves 4-6.

Chicken with Capers

3 Tbsp. OLIVE OIL
1 clove GARLIC, minced
4 boneless, skinless CHICKEN BREASTS
JUICE from 1 - 2 FRESH LEMONS
1/2 cup dry WHITE WINE
BLACK PEPPER, freshly ground
2 Tbsp. CAPERS

Heat oil in frying pan. Gently sauté garlic. Add chicken and cook over medium high heat until chicken begins to brown. Squeeze lemon over chicken and add white wine. Sprinkle liberally with pepper. Cook for approximately 10 minutes. During the last minute of cooking time, add capers.

Serves 4.

National Beef Cook-Off® Recipes

Ranching has been one of the mainstays of the Colorado economy since the days of the early cowboys. In 1952 a network of women in the beef industry concerned with educating consumers formed the American National Cowbelles. Based in Denver, the organization was designed to give women a strong voice in the beef industry. In 1987, the organization changed its name to the American National CattleWomen to reflect a more contemporary image. Since 1974, the American National CattleWomen have sponsored the National Beef Cook-Off to generate an awareness of the versatility, convenience and great taste of beef. The two recipes that follow are winning recipes. Created by Colorado cooks, both recipes are ideal for holiday entertaining.

Spanish Steak with Sautéed Vegetables

National Beef Cook-Off®

1 lb. BEEF TOP SIRLOIN STEAK, trimmed, boned and cut
    3/4 inch thick
1 tsp. GARLIC POWDER, divided
1/4 tsp. BLACK PEPPER, freshly ground
2 tsp. VEGETABLE OIL, divided
1 tsp. BUTTER
3/4 tsp. SALT, divided
1 each med. RED AND GREEN BELL PEPPER,
    cut lengthwise into thin strips
1 small ONION, thinly sliced
1 cup fresh MUSHROOMS, sliced
1/3 cup WALNUTS, chopped
1/4 tsp. CHILI POWDER
1 Tbsp. SOUR CREAM
2 Tbsp. canned GREEN CHILES, drained and chopped
LEMON SLICES
CILANTRO SPRIGS

(See directions on next page)

Pound beef steak with flat side of meat mallet to about 1/4-inch thickness. Combine 1/2 teaspoon garlic powder and pepper; sprinkle over steak. Heat 1 teaspoon oil and butter in 12-inch heavy frying pan over medium-high heat until hot. Pan-fry steak 5 to 7 minutes for medium-rare or to desired doneness, turning once. Remove steak to heated platter; sprinkle with 1/2 teaspoon salt. Keep warm. Add remaining 1 teaspoon oil to frying pan. Add red and green peppers, onion, mushrooms and walnuts. Cook 2 minutes, stirring frequently. Combine remaining 1/2 teaspoon garlic powder, 1/4 teaspoon salt and chili powder; sprinkle over vegetables and continue cooking 2 minutes, stirring frequently. Spread steak with sour cream; top with chiles. Starting at short side, roll up steak jelly-roll fashion; secure with 4 wooden picks. Spoon vegetables around steak roll; garnish with lemon slices and cilantro sprigs. To serve, carve steak roll between wooden picks; remove and discard wooden picks.

Serves 4.

Savory Roast Beef with Glazed Carrots

*Recipe provided courtesy of the National Beef Cook-Off®
sponsored by the American National CattleWomen.*

3 - 4 lb. BEEF TENDERLOIN ROAST, well trimmed
1 1/2 Tbsp. OLIVE OIL
1 1/4 tsp. GARLIC SALT
1 tsp. dried OREGANO LEAVES
1/2 tsp. each PAPRIKA and freshly ground BLACK PEPPER
2 Tbsp. ALL-PURPOSE FLOUR
1 1/2 cups BEEF BOUILLON
PEPPER (optional)
PARSLEY, minced

Brush roast all over with olive oil. Combine garlic salt, oregano, paprika and pepper; sprinkle evenly over roast. Place roast on rack in shallow roasting pan. Insert meat thermometer so bulb is centered in thickest part of roast. Do not add water. Do not cover. Roast in 350 degree oven 45 to 60 minutes for rare (135 degrees) to medium rare (145 degrees). Remove to carving board; tent with foil and let stand 10 minutes. Temperature of roast will continue to rise about 5 degrees to 140 degrees F for rare or 150 degrees for medium rare.

Meanwhile prepare **Glazed Carrots** (see recipe on next page); keep warm. While roast is standing, cook 2 tablespoons pan juices and flour over medium-low heat for 2 minutes; stirring constantly. (If necessary, add melted butter or margarine to pan juices to equal 2 tablespoons.) Add beef bouillon; bring to a boil and cook until thickened, stirring constantly. Season with pepper to taste, if desired. Carve roast into thin slices; arrange on serving platter. Spoon some of gravy over roast; serve with remaining gravy and **Glazed Carrots**. Sprinkle roast and carrots with parsley.

Serves 12.

(Continued next page)

Glazed Carrots

8 med. CARROTS, cut into 2-inch pieces
2/3 cup WATER
2 Tbsp. BUTTER or MARGARINE
1 Tbsp. packed BROWN SUGAR
1/2 tsp. INSTANT BEEF BOUILLON GRANULES
dash of PEPPER

Combine carrots, water, butter, brown sugar, bouillon granules and pepper in medium saucepan. Bring to a boil; reduce heat. Cover and simmer 20 minutes or until carrots are tender. Uncover and boil over high heat 5 minutes or until sauce has reduced to a glaze, stirring frequently.

Makes about 4 cups.

CHAPTER SIX

Pikes Peak or Bust!

When the United States was in its infancy, Lt. Zebulon Pike was dispatched to discover what lay in the vast reaches of the West that had been acquired three years earlier in the Louisiana Purchase of 1803. Four months into his journey he sighted a magnificent mountain in the distance. He reckoned it was a day's trip away. Two weeks later he arrived at his elusive destination. Undeterred by the frustrations of his lengthy trip, he was determined to climb to the summit. Though he failed to reach the top, he nevertheless earned a place in history for his discovery.

Heeding the call of the frontier, thousands eventually followed in Pikes's footsteps. Lured by the promise of gold, "Pikes Peak or Bust" became their motto.

After the gold rush, Pikes Peak was still a magnet for those drawn by its magnificent vistas. One such visitor was Katharine Lee Bates, an English professor at Wellesley College, who was spend-  ing the summer of 1893 as a visiting professor at Colorado College. Overwhelmed by the beauty surrounding her as she looked out from atop the mountain, she penned the words to a poem — "America the Beautiful." Though it was several years before the poem appeared in print, once published it was soon put to music.

The emotions experienced by Professor Bates are shared by the thousands who visit Pikes Peak every spring, summer, fall and winter. Each season offers its own distinctive beauty, but during the holidays Pikes Peak takes on a special meaning. On New Year's Eve, Pikes Peak is the site of a fabulous fireworks display to ring in the New Year.

Side Dishes

Baked Acorn Squash with Pineapple Glaze

1 ACORN SQUASH, cut in half
2 tsp. BUTTER, divided
SALT
PEPPER
4 Tbsp. CRUSHED PINEAPPLE, drained
2 tsp. BROWN SUGAR
1 Tbsp. slivered almonds
1 Tbsp. MARASCHINO CHERRIES, chopped
2 tsp. CHERRY JUICE
2 tsp. ORANGE JUICE

Wash and cut acorn squash in half. Scrape out seeds and coarse pulp. Rub each inside with butter, and salt and pepper to taste. Place cut side down in well greased baking pan. Bake in hot oven at 400 degrees for 30 minutes. While squash is baking, mix together crushed pineapple, brown sugar, slivered almonds, maraschino cherries and juices.

Turn squash over and fill each half with pineapple mixture. Cover pan and continue baking until squash middles are done, about 30 minutes. Remove from oven. Cover with **Pineapple Glaze**.

Pineapple Glaze

1 cup PINEAPPLE JUICE
1 tsp. grated ORANGE RIND
1 tsp. grated LIME RIND
1 1/2 Tbsp. CORN STARCH
1 Tbsp. BROWN SUGAR

Blend ingredients over medium heat. Stir until thick. Let stand for 5 to 7 minutes. Pour evenly over each half of the filled cooked squash.

Scalloped Broccoli

A tasty addition to any Christmas feast. This dish can be prepared in advance and refrigerated.

**1 lg. bunch BROCCOLI, cut into stalks, and
    cooked until tender crisp
1/4 cup minced ONION
1/4 cup BUTTER, melted
1/4 cup FLOUR
1 tsp. SALT
1/8 tsp. PEPPER
2 cups MILK
1 1/2 cups grated CHEDDAR CHEESE
1/2 cup buttered BREAD CRUMBS**

Cook onion in butter until tender. Add flour and seasonings, blend. Add milk, and cook until thickened, stirring constantly. Remove from heat and stir in cheese. Alternate layers of broccoli and sauce in buttered 2-quart casserole. Top with bread crumbs and bake in a 350 degree oven for 20 minutes or until lightly browned.

Asparagus with Parmesan

**1 cup CHICKEN BROTH
1 bunch ASPARAGUS, trimmed
Fresh LEMON JUICE to taste
2 - 3 Tbsp. PARMESAN CHEESE, freshly grated**

Bring chicken broth to a boil in a frying pan. Add asparagus, cover and simmer about 7 minutes, or until desired doneness. Drain, remove from pan and add lemon juice and Parmesan cheese.

Serves 4.

Old Fashioned Cranberries

1 bag fresh CRANBERRIES
RUM, as desired
BROWN SUGAR

Wash cranberries and place in small casserole dish. Pour rum over top and cover liberally with brown sugar. Cover and cook in 350 degree oven for 1 hour or until berries are soft.

Festive Holiday Stir-Fry

1 ZUCCHINI
1 YELLOW CROOKNECK SQUASH
1 RED PEPPER
OLIVE OIL
1 clove GARLIC, finely chopped

Slice squash and pepper into julienne strips about two inches long. Pour enough olive oil to just lightly cover bottom of medium-sized frying pan. Heat oil slightly and add garlic and vegetables. Sauté over medium high heat until tender, about 8 minutes.

Spicy Green Beans

At Christmas time, it's hard to be concerned with watching cholesterol or calories, but here's a fairly healthy dish to complement any holiday dinner.

1 lb. GREEN BEANS
1 LEMON
MARGARINE
EXTRA SPICY MRS. DASH®

Snap off the ends of the green beans and wash. Drop into boiling water and cook until desired doneness, roughly 8 - 10 minutes for slightly crunchy. Drain and return to pot and squeeze lemon over all. Add a touch of margarine and a generous shake of Mrs. Dash.

Garlic Mashed Potatoes

A garlicky twist for a holiday classic.

6 md. RED POTATOES
1/2 - 3/4 cup warm MILK
4 Tbsp. BUTTER or MARGARINE
2 - 3 cloves GARLIC, finely chopped
SALT
PEPPER

Peel and quarter the potatoes. Place in pan and cover with cold water. Bring to a boil and gently boil for about 20 minutes, or until tender when pierced with a fork. Drain well and return to pan. Gradually add warm milk, butter and garlic and mix with electric beater until lumps are gone. Add salt and pepper to taste.

Sweet Potato Casserole

4 md. SWEET POTATOES
1 Tbsp. BUTTER or MARGARINE
1/3 cup ORANGE JUICE
2 Tbsp. WALNUTS, chopped
1/4 tsp. NUTMEG
SALT
PEPPER

Boil whole sweet potatoes for 25 to 30 minutes, or until tender. Drain, peel potatoes when cool and mash. Add remaining ingredients and mix well. Place in a 1-quart buttered casserole dish and bake, uncovered, for 25 minutes at 375 degrees.

Christmas Zucchini with Tomatoes

Green zucchini paired with red tomatoes makes this a colorful dish for Christmas dinner.

2 ZUCCHINI, sliced
1 - 2 cloves GARLIC, minced
2 Tbsp. OLIVE OIL
1 can (14 1/2 oz.) S&W® Ready-Cut Italian Style Tomatoes
1/4 - 1/2 tsp. BASIL LEAVES
1/4 - 1/2 tsp. OREGANO LEAVES
1/4 - 1/2 tsp. PEPPER

Sauté the zucchini and garlic in the olive oil for about 5 minutes. Add the tomatoes, along with roughly half of the juice, and the seasonings; gently simmer until zucchini is done to taste.

Cranberries a l'Orange

2 cups SUGAR
2 cups WATER
1 lb. fresh CRANBERRIES
3 Tbsp. GRAND MARNIER
Grated ORANGE PEEL of 1 ORANGE
JUICE from 1 sm. LEMON
2 Tbsp. SUGAR

Combine sugar and water. Boil for 5 minutes. Add cranberries and boil an additional five minutes until almost jelled. Fold in remaining ingredients. Remove from heat. Sprinkle with 2 tablespoons sugar. Chill.

Apple Rings

Easy to prepare and a wonderful accompaniment to roast pork, these tasty apples are also a good snack after an afternoon of ice skating or sledding.

3 - 4 APPLES
2 1/2 Tbsp. BUTTER
3 Tbsp. BROWN SUGAR
1 tsp. CINNAMON

Peel and core apples. Cut into 1/2-inch thick rings. Melt butter in a frying pan and add brown sugar and cinnamon. Sauté apples, turning to coat evenly. Cover and cook over low heat for 10 to 15 minutes, stirring occasionally.

Oyster Stuffing

2 Tbsp. BUTTER
1 lb. SAUSAGE
1/2 cup ONIONS, finely chopped
1/4 cup CELERY, finely chopped
1/3 cup GREEN BELL PEPPER, finely chopped
1/3 cup RED BELL PEPPER, finely chopped
1/4 cup GREEN ONIONS, finely chopped
1 clove GARLIC, finely chopped
1 jar (8-10 oz.) OYSTERS
1/4 tsp. THYME
1/2 tsp. SAGE
1/4 tsp. ROSEMARY
1/2 BLACK PEPPER, freshly ground
3 cups coarse BREAD CRUMBS
1 cup CHICKEN STOCK, OYSTER LIQUID
TABASCO® to taste
SALT to taste

Melt butter in large frying pan over medium high heat. Add sausage and cook 5 minutes. Lower heat to medium and add onions and celery. Cook about 10 minutes. Add green and red peppers, green onions and garlic. Cook an additional 5 minutes. Meanwhile, drain oysters, reserving liquid. Add oysters to sausage and vegetable mixture and cook for 2 minutes. Remove from heat and add thyme, sage, rosemary, black pepper and bread crumbs. Mix well. Moisten stuffing with reserved oyster liquid and chicken stock to make mixture moist but not soggy. Add salt and Tabasco. Mix well. Place in baking dish and bake uncovered for 20 minutes at 350 degrees.

CHAPTER SEVEN

Christmas in Denver

Today and Yesterday

Denver has something for everyone during the Christmas season, beginning with the annual lighting of the star atop Castle Rock in mid-November.

Denver itself becomes a festival of lights during the holidays. The City and County Building is awash in lights, billing itself as the "World's Largest Christmas Lighting Display," the Botanic Gardens becomes a wonderland filled with giant flowers of lights, and the Denver Zoo creates a menagerie of animals made of lights. On Christmas Eve, a parade of skiers weave their way down the snow-covered slopes of Winter Park Resort in a trail of twinkling lights.

For many, the holidays would not be complete without a visit to the Brown Palace, its atrium transformed into a winter wonderland of greenery and lights. Other festivities include the Annual Holiday Food and Gift Festival at Currigan Exhibition Hall, the Festival of Trees at the Radisson Hotel, and the Colorado Children's Chorale at Boettcher Concert Hall.

For those interested in a step back in time, a Victorian Christmas can be celebrated every weekend in December at Larimer Square, amid strolling carolers and roasting chestnuts. Father Christmas himself even puts in an appearance.

In addition, Four Mile Historic Park hosts an annual holiday open house featuring cookie baking in a wood stove, old fashioned ornaments, sleigh rides, and a visit with St.

Nick. The Four Mile House is Denver's oldest standing house, situated on a 14-acre living history farm. In the 1860s the house served as a stage stop on the Cherokee Trail, where innkeeper Mary Cawker served stew and dried apple pie to the gold-seeking travelers who stopped there.

In 1864 Mary sold the house to Levi and Millie Booth, and in 1883 they built a brick Victorian addition onto the 1859 log house. The menu below is an authentic representation of foods that would have been included in their Victorian Christmas dinner.

Christmas Menu

(C. 1883 for the Booth Family)

Stewed Oysters

Boned Turkey • *Stuffed Ham*

Mashed Potatoes

Turnips • *Beets* • *Fried Celery*

Gelatin with Fruits and Nuts

Candied Sweet Potatoes

Plum Pudding

Baked Lemon Pudding

Fruit Cake

Nuts

Candied Oranges

Coffee

Desserts

Dried Apple Pie

This recipe, provided courtesy of Four Mile Historic Park, was served at Four Mile House between 1860 and 1885. Pioneer cooks did not usually prebake pie shells as we do today. They expected the bottom crust to absorb juices and greased the pie pan to prevent the wet crust from sticking.

Cook **one pound DRIED APPLES** in one quart of water for 30-45 minutes or soak them overnight.

Combine the following and sift over the apples:

1/2 cup white SUGAR
1/8 tsp. SALT
1/4 tsp. CINNAMON

Stir gently until the apples are coated. Place apples in a pie shell, cover with top crust, crimp and vent. Bake at 425 degrees, then reduce heat to 350 degrees and bake until the pie is nicely browned, about 40 minutes. Cool at least one hour before serving.

Double Crust:

2 1/2 cups FLOUR
1 tsp. SALT
2/3 cups LARD
1 tsp. BUTTER

Prepare a cup of ice water. Mix flour and salt in the bowl. Spoon the lard in the flour and blend until the mixture is coarse. Continue to toss as you add 3 tablespoons of ice water. Press the dough into two balls and chill.

Dust pastry surface with flour and flatten dough on it. Roll the dough into a circle 2 inches wider than the pan and 1/8 inch thick. Fold the dough into quarters and place in buttered pie pan. Unfold dough and trim around pan edge. Roll out the other half of the dough. After filling the bottom crust, moisten its rim. Place the top crust on the pie and trim the edges. Pinch the edges of both crust together. Vent the top crust by slashing it in a simple design.

Christmas Carrot Cake

1 1/2 cup sifted FLOUR
1 tsp. BAKING POWDER
1 tsp. BAKING SODA
1/2 tsp. each SALT, CINNAMON, and NUTMEG
1/2 cup WHOLE CRANBERRY SAUCE
1 cup SUGAR
2/3 cup VEGETABLE OIL
2 EGGS, slightly beaten
1 cup CARROTS, shredded
1/2 cup POWDERED SUGAR
1 tbsp. LIGHT CREAM

Sift together flour, baking powder, baking soda, salt and spices. Add cranberry sauce, sugar, oil and slightly beaten eggs. Mix. Add shredded carrots. Pour into greased and floured 9 x 9 x 2 pan. Bake at 350 degrees for 40-45 minutes. Before serving, combine powdered sugar and light cream. Drizzle over cake. Top with sprig of holly or parsley. Serves 8-10 people.

Sherry Poppy Seed Cake

1 pkg. YELLOW CAKE MIX
1 pkg. VANILLA PUDDING (not instant)
3/4 cup VEGETABLE OIL
3/4 cup SHERRY
1 tsp. VANILLA
1 tsp. NUTMEG
4 EGGS
1/3 cup POPPY SEEDS

Mix all ingredients and bake at 350 degrees in a greased Bundt pan for 40 minutes.

Slovakian Prune Cake

"This cake recipe was my husband's grandfather's, who was lovingly called "Dedo." He brought it with him to America when he immigrated at age 17 in 1906. The family loves this recipe for the holidays. I prefer the flavor of the cake without a heavy frosting, so I enjoy putting the rum glaze over it. Those who do not care for the rum can simply increase the water by 1/4 cup. It is a moist spice cake. No high altitude adjustments are necessary." Barbara Sabol, Cascade

2 cups FLOUR
1 cup SUGAR
1/2 cup BROWN SUGAR, packed
1 1/4 tsp. BAKING SODA
2 tsp. each NUTMEG, ALLSPICE and CINNAMON
1 cup BLACK WALNUTS, chopped; or any other NUTMEATS
3 EGGS
3/4 cup VEGETABLE OIL
1 cup BUTTERMILK
1 cup cooked PRUNES, pitted, then whipped with a mixer

Stir together dry ingredients. Mix well all liquid ingredients in a separate bowl. Combine all ingredients and mix well. Pour into greased and floured 10-inch Bundt cake pan. Bake in a 325-degree oven for 45 minutes.

Rum Glaze

1 stick MARGARINE   **1/4 cup RUM**
1/2 cup WATER   **1 cup SUGAR**

During the last 10 minutes of baking time, bring all the ingredients to a three minute boil. Pour the syrup over the hot cake, saving a little for the top when you turn the cake out of the pan.

Tip: Don't let the cake cool too long, or the syrup will cause it to stick to the pan.

Holiday Pudding with Brandy Sauce

3 cups MILK, scalded
1 1/4 cups SALTINES, rolled
1 cup SUGAR
3 EGGS, slightly beaten
1 tsp. NUTMEG or MIXED SPICES
1 tsp. SALT
1/3 cup BUTTER, melted
3/4 cup WALNUTS
1 cup RAISINS, parboiled to soften

Pour scalded milk over the rolled crackers. Let stand until cool. Mix sugar and slightly beaten eggs, spices, salt, butter and nuts. Add this to cooled cracker mixture. Mix. Add the partially softened parboiled raisins to cracker mixture. Turn into a well-buttered 2 1/2 quart casserole. Bake at 325 degrees for 1 hour. Serve warm with **Brandy Sauce.**

Serves 8-10 people.

Brandy Sauce

1 cup SUGAR
2 tablespoons CORNSTARCH
2 cups WATER
2 tablespoons BUTTER
2 teaspoons BRANDY to taste

Mix sugar, cornstarch and water. Add butter and cook in a saucepan until thickened. Remove from stove and add the brandy. Stir. Serve warm over the **Holiday Pudding.**

Note: Vanilla may be substituted for the brandy.

Blueberry Crisp

Because it's made with blueberries, which are usually not eaten year round, this scrumptious dessert is all the more special at Christmas.

1/2 cup SUGAR
3 Tbsp. CORNSTARCH
2 tsp. ground CINNAMON
4 cups fresh or frozen BLUEBERRIES
2 cups TART APPLES, sliced and peeled
1/2 cup packed BROWN SUGAR
1/4 cup quick-cooking OATMEAL
3 Tbsp. all purpose FLOUR
2 Tbsp. BUTTER or MARGARINE, melted
1/2 cup PECANS, chopped
VANILLA ICE CREAM

Preheat oven to 350 degrees. Butter an 8 1/2 x 2 inch-round baking dish. In a large bowl, mix sugar, cornstarch and 1 teaspoon of the cinnamon. Add blueberries and apples; toss until evenly coated. Place in baking dish and set aside. In a medium bowl, mix brown sugar, oatmeal, flour, and remaining teaspoon of cinnamon. Stir in butter until evenly moistened. Stir in pecans. Spoon over the fruit mixture and bake 45 minutes or until bubbly and apples are tender. Cool 10 minutes before serving. Top with ice cream. Serves 6.

For many families, Christmas would not be complete without a trip to the elegant Broadmoor in Colorado Springs. These next three recipes are holiday favorites at the Broadmoor.

Rum Cake with Rum Syrup

3 oz. SUGAR
8 oz. BUTTER
1/4 oz. SALT
Dash LEMON ZEST
Dash VANILLA
8 EGGS
1 lb. 4 oz. FLOUR
1 1/4 oz. BAKING POWDER
6 oz. RAISINS
ALMONDS

Cream sugar, butter, salt, lemon zest and vanilla. Add eggs, two by two, scraping the sides of the bowl from time to time. Sift flour with baking powder. Combine flour with creamed mixture. Add raisins and stir. Pour into greased kouglof mold and sprinkle with almonds. Bake at 360 degrees for approximately 45 minutes. Remove cake from pan while hot. Allow to cool slightly, then dip warm cake into warm **Rum Syrup**.

Rum Syrup

6 oz. SUGAR
1 qt. WATER
1 ORANGE SLICE
2 oz. MEYERS® RUM

Bring sugar, water and orange slice to a boil. Cool to 100 degrees. Add rum. Dip cake quickly into syrup. Drain on screen.

Bread Pudding

The Broadmoor

1 loaf FRENCH BREAD, sliced
Approximately 1 oz. MELTED BUTTER
10 EGGS
9 oz. SUGAR
1 1/4 qt. MILK
3 oz. RAISINS
Pinch SALT
Pinch CINNAMON
Few drops VANILLA FLAVORING

Grease a 9 x 12 baking pan. Pour melted butter lightly over the bread. Mix eggs, sugar, milk and raisins. Add spices and vanilla. Pour over bread. Bake at 350 degrees in a water bath until firm.

English Vanilla Custard Cream

The Broadmoor

1 qt. MILK, scalded
1 Tbsp. VANILLA
12 EGG YOLKS
3/4 cup SUGAR
1/4 cup MEYERS® RUM or to taste (optional)

Heat milk and vanilla. Beat egg yolks slightly and mix with sugar. Pour hot milk over sugar/egg yolk mixture gradually. Stir rapidly to blend all ingredients. Place over hot water bath and cook for approximately 10 minutes or until the mixture begins to thicken and coat the spoon. **Do not boil!** Can be served hot or cold.

Applesauce Jar Cake

Fun to make, these cakes are very good and make wonderful Christmas gifts.

2/3 cup SHORTENING
2 2/3 cups SUGAR
4 EGGS
2 cups APPLESAUCE
2/3 cups WATER
3 1/3 cups FLOUR
1/2 tsp. BAKING POWDER

2 tsp. BAKING SODA
1/2 tsp. SALT
1 tsp.CINNAMON
1/2 tsp. CLOVES
2/3 cup NUTMEATS and/or
    RAISINS, CANDIED FRUIT

Cream together shortening and sugar; add eggs, beating well after each addition. Stir in applesauce and water. Sift together the flour, baking powder, baking soda, salt, cinnamon, and cloves. Stir dry ingredients into applesauce mixture. Add nuts, raisins, or candied fruit. Pour into straight-sided, wide-mouthed canning jars. Fill 1/2 full; bake at 325 degrees for 35-40 minutes. Remove, one at a time from the oven, wipe rim clean, and seal with a lid. They can be stored on a shelf, but refrigerate after opening. The jars sometimes seal very tight and are hard to open. If necessary, punch a hole in the lid to break the vacuum. Yield: 9 pints.

Cranberry Ice

1 pkg. GELATIN
3 cups SUGAR
3 cups WATER

1 qt. CRANBERRIES,
    cooked
JUICE FROM 3 LEMONS

Combine gelatin, sugar and water. Bring to a boil. Cover cranberries with plenty of water and boil 10 to 15 minutes. Strain cooked cranberries through a sieve or colander. Combine cranberries, gelatin and lemon juice. Pour into 6, 3-oz. paper cups and freeze.

Olde English Plum Pudding

A Christmas classic that's well worth the time and effort!

6 EGGS
1 qt. SWEET MILK
1 heaping pt. GROUND SUET
1 box SEEDED RAISINS
1 box CURRANTS
2/3 SUGAR
1 scant tsp. BAKING SODA
1 tsp. CINNAMON
1/2 tsp. ALLSPICE
1/2 tsp. CLOVES
FLOUR to make a thick batter

Combine all ingredients, adding enough flour to make a thick batter. Pour batter in greased 1-pound coffee cans, filling about 3/4 full and cover with aluminum foil. Place cans in large pot (canning pot, lobster pot) and fill pot with water halfway up the cans. Boil 3 to 4 hours. Cool in refrigerator (or outside in the snow). When ready to serve remove from cans and cut into 1/2-inch slices. Steam the slices in a double boiler. Serve with **Pudding Sauce**.

Yield: 4 - 1 pound coffee cans.

Pudding Sauce

1/2 cup BUTTER
1 cup SUGAR
1 tsp. VANILLA
1 Tbsp. FLOUR
1/2 cup SWEET CREAM
1 1/2 Tbsp. BRANDY

Combine all ingredients except brandy in a saucepan and heat over low heat. Add brandy before serving over **Plum Pudding**.

Christmas Strawberry Rice Pie

1 9-inch BAKED PIE SHELL
1 pkg. (8-oz.) CREAM CHEESE, softened
1/2 cup SUGAR
1 1/2 cup FROZEN STRAWBERRIES, thawed
1 1/2 tsp. unflavored GELATIN
4 Tbsp. JUICE from the strawberries
1 cup RICE, cooked
1/2 pint HEAVY CREAM, whipped

Mix cream cheese and sugar until light and fluffy. Add strawberries. Dissolve gelatin in heated juice from strawberries. Combine with cream cheese mixture and cooked rice, and mix well. Fold in whipped cream. Turn into baked pie shell and chill 3 hours.

Note: Raspberries can be substituted for strawberries. A graham cracker pie crust also works well.

Chocolate Sauce

Here's an effortless way to turn ice cream or pudding into a special dessert.

3 cups SUGAR
1 1/4 cups HERSHEY'S® COCOA
1 cup hot strong COFFEE
1 can CONDENSED MILK
1/8 lb. BUTTER

Mix all ingredients together. Heat gently in double boiler or a saucepan until velvety. Serve hot on ice cream or pudding.

CHAPTER EIGHT

The Season of Giving

Christmas is a time of gathering with friends and family to join together for a fabulous feast, but of all the traditions associated with Christmas, the oldest of all is giving. It is, of course, a time for exchanging gifts as well as warm wishes for the coming year.

In the spirit of the season, our thoughts often turn to those less fortunate. As reported on the front page of the *Denver Post* on December 22, 1920, Coloradans were looking after each other.

Free Rabbits for the Poor Folk!

Cottontails, jack rabbits — all free to the needy of Denver! Watch Thursday's Denver Post. It will tell you where and when you can get a fine, fresh fat rabbit free for your Christmas dinner.

The hunters are on the job Wednesday. More than 100 scatter gun experts are taking part in the American Legion-Denver Post hunt in the vicinity of Wiggins, Colorado. All the rabbits they shoot will be brought to Denver for distribution by The Post among the poor people of Denver.

When the United States was at war with Germany no one was too poor to contribute something to make the hard life of the soldiers just a little more pleasant. The ex-service men and a squad of marines from the Denver recruiting office area are doing their best Wednesday to repay some of the kindnesses they received during the war. They are going to see to it that no family in Denver lacks for meat for its Christmas dinner.

This spirit still prevails and can be seen on people's faces as they welcome loved ones to their homes for the holidays, as they exchange gifts with friends, and as they join in the many family and community traditions that abound throughout the state as Coloradans celebrate the season.

Cookies, Candies & Bars

Krollettes

Krollettes are Christmas cookies originating in Sweden. After locating in Pueblo, Donald Gleason modified an old recipe and came up with these tasty goodies. Each year he makes about 60 dozen to share with neighbors, lodge brothers and friends, who eagerly await the next Christmas.

4 EGGS
2 Tbsp. SUGAR
1/2 Tsp. SALT
2 cups WHOLE MILK
2 cups FLOUR
2 tsp. VANILLA
1 gal. VEGETABLE OIL
POWDERED SUGAR

Equipment required for this recipe: rosette iron (either single or double) with handle, deep fryer, small flat aluminum baking pan (large enough to fit double iron), table fork, gravy ladle.

Pour oil into deep fat fryer. Set temperature control to 360 degrees. While oil is heating, place paper toweling on counter or large board to place cookies after removing from oil. Place iron in oil to heat. Beat eggs slightly in mixer bowl with sugar and salt. Mix flour and milk in blender until smooth. Combine with egg mixture and vanilla, beating only until smooth. Dip enough batter into flat pan to cover bottom and sides of rosette iron when immersed.

Remove iron from hot oil, drain, dip into batter, being careful to coat only bottom and sides, immerse in hot oil for about 1 1/2 minutes or until golden brown. Remove from oil, tip to drain, pry Krollette from iron with fork, dip iron into batter and repeat. After cooling, just before serving, coat with powdered sugar. These will keep about a month, uncovered, protected by paper toweling or cloth.

Note: One gallon of oil will make about 60 dozen Krollettes.

Pueblo boasts one of the state's finest examples of Victorian architecture — the Rosemount Victorian House Museum. At Christmas time this 24,000-square foot mansion recreates a Victorian Christmas with its "Dickens of a Christmas" celebration. The house is adorned with Victorian era decorations, with one room featuring likenesses of Scrooge and Bob Cratchit.

Lorraine's Franklin House B & B Date Nut Bars

"These date nut bars have been a tradition in our family since day one. The Franklin House B & B serves them to their guests every Christmas, and everyone wants the recipe. Occasionally, we write the recipe in German, French, or Spanish—not an easy task," writes George Bauer, the innkeeper of Franklin House Bed & Breakfast, a charming 1890s Queen Anne Victorian house located in Denver. This recipe was handed down to him from his great grandmother.

3/4 cup FLOUR
1/2 cup ALL BRAN
1 cup NUTS, chopped
1 cup DATES, chopped
3/4 tsp. BAKING POWDER
1/4 tsp. SALT
3 EGGS
1 1/2 cup BROWN SUGAR
1 tsp. VANILLA
POWDERED SUGAR

Sift and measure the flour. Add bran, nuts, dates, baking powder and salt. Beat eggs and add sugar and vanilla. Stir in flour mixture. Spread 1/2 inch thick in greased pan. Bake at 375 degrees for 20 minutes. Cut into squares while warm and coat with powdered sugar—twice.

Note: Recipe may be doubled.

White Christmas Fudge

This tasty fudge adds color variety to a plate of chocolate fudge.

2 cups SUGAR
1/2 cup SOUR CREAM
1/3 cup WHITE CORN SYRUP
2 Tbsp. BUTTER
1/2 tsp. SALT
1 tsp. VANILLA
1/2 tsp. RUM EXTRACT
1/4 cup CANDIED CHERRIES, quartered
1 cup WALNUTS, chopped

Combine sugar, sour cream, corn syrup, butter and salt in a saucepan. Bring to a boil slowly, stirring until sugar dissolves. Boil without stirring to 226 degrees or soft ball stage. Remove from heat and let stand for 15 minutes. Do not stir. Add vanilla and rum extract and beat until mixture starts to lose gloss. Stir in candied cherries and walnuts. Cut into squares.

Yield: 1 pound.

The Twelve Days of Christmas

A partridge in a pear tree . . .

Two turtle doves . . .

Fattigmann Bakkels

A Norwegian delicacy. Fun to make and fun to eat at the holidays.

1 gal. VEGETABLE OIL
4 EGGS
4 Tbsp. SOUR CREAM
4 Tbsp. SUGAR
1 tsp. VANILLA
1/8 tsp. SALT
2 1/2 cups FLOUR

Equipment required for this recipe: bread board, rolling pin, sharp knife, deep fryer, slotted spoon, paper toweling.

Pour oil into deep fryer. Set temperature control to 370 degrees. Beat eggs until thick. Add sour cream, sugar, vanilla, salt and gradually add flour. Roll out on bread board very thin. Cut into triangles. Make a slit in the long side of the triangle. Then put the opposite point through the slit, making a cylinder. Fry in deep fat at 370 degrees. Turn frequently until golden brown. Remove with a slotted spoon and place on paper toweling to drain and cool.

Yield: About 2 dozen.

Three French hens . . .

Four calling birds . . .

Date Nut Roll Candy

This date nut roll candy is fun to make and eat.

1 1/2 cups BROWN SUGAR
1 1/2 cups WHITE SUGAR
3/4 cup CREAM
1/8 tsp. SALT
1 lb. PITTED DATES
1 cup NUTMEATS, chopped
1 tsp. VANILLA

Mix sugars, cream, and salt. Cook in saucepan to melt and boil to soft ball stage, tested in cold water, stirring constantly. Add 1 pound dates and boil, stirring constantly until it reaches the firm ball stage. Add cup of nutmeats and 1 teaspoon of vanilla. Remove from fire; set pan in cold water and cool to lukewarm. Turn onto board dusted thickly with powdered sugar and knead until it will mold well. Roll to 1 inch in diameter and let stand 24 hours. Slice to serve.

Yield: 2 pounds.

Five gold rings . . .

Six geese a'laying . . .

Granny Fitz's Nut Cups

*A long-time family favorite from Jane Yerkman
of Blackhawk.*

Crust Mixture:

1 pkg. (3 ozs.) CREAM CHEESE
1 stick BUTTER or MARGARINE
1 cup FLOUR

Mix together well; form into a ball, using hands, and wrap in waxed paper. Refrigerate overnight or at least 8 hours.

Filling:

1 EGG, beaten
3/4 cup DARK BROWN SUGAR
1 Tbsp. BUTTER
1 tsp. VANILLA
1/2 cup PECANS, chopped

Beat together all ingredients except pecans. Stir in pecans. In small (1 x 1) muffin tins, form small amount of crust mixture as if making a pie shell. With a spoon, fill each shell with filling mixture. Bake at 350 degrees for 25 to 30 minutes.

Remove shells and let sit on several layers of paper towels for 2 to 3 hours. Sprinkle with powdered sugar.

Seven swans a'swimming . . .   *Eight maids a'milking . . .*

Chocolate Chunk White Chocolate Chip Cookies

A favorite for holiday open houses and afternoon tea. Sallie and Welling Clark, innkeepers of The Holden House 1902 Bed & Breakfast Inn of Colorado Springs, offer their guests a bottomless Cookie Jar filled with these scrumptious cookies.

3/4 cup BROWN SUGAR
3/4 cup BUTTER or MARGARINE
2 EGGS
1 tsp. VANILLA
2 1/2 cups FLOUR
1 tsp. BAKING SODA
1/2 pkg. of 12 ounce CHOCOLATE CHUNKS
1/2 pkg. of 10 ounce HERSHEY'S® VANILLA CHIPS
1/4 cup WALNUTS, chopped

Preheat oven to 375 to 400 degrees. Soften brown sugar and butter in microwave for 1 minute on high. Add eggs and vanilla. Mix well. Add flour and baking soda to sugar/egg mixture. When well mixed, add chocolate chunks, vanilla chips, and walnuts. Place well-rounded teaspoonful on ungreased insulated cookie sheet. Bake for 10-12 minutes or until slightly brown on top.

Yield: approximately 2 dozen.

Nine ladies dancing . . .

Ten lords a'leaping . . .

Jello Pudding Cookies

A quick and easy recipe!

1 stick MARGARINE
1/2 cup BROWN SUGAR, packed
2 EGGS
1 cup PEANUT BUTTER
1 tsp. VANILLA
1 cup COCONUT
1 cup FLOUR
1/2 tsp. SALT
1 cup OATS
1 tsp. BAKING POWDER
1 pkg. (sm. size) INSTANT JELLO® PUDDING
1 cup CHOCOLATE CHIPS

Mix first six ingredients together and set aside. Then mix next five ingredients together and add to first mixture. Add chocolate chips. Drop onto ungreased cookie sheet. Bake at 350 degrees for 12-15 minutes or until lightly browned.

Yield: 3 dozen.

Eleven pipers piping . . .   Twelve drummers drumming . . .

French Lemon Bars

These elegant bars are absolutely irresistible — but they are rich, so cut them into small squares.

3/4 cup cold BUTTER
1/3 cup POWDERED SUGAR
1 1/2 cups FLOUR
3 EGGS

1 1/2 cups SUGAR
1 Tbsp. FLOUR
3 Tbsp. LEMON JUICE
POWDERED SUGAR, for dusti

Cream butter with powdered sugar until blended. Add flour and cut in with a pastry blender until crumbly. Pat into a 13 x 9 pan and bake at 350 degrees for 20 minutes. Meanwhile, beat the eggs and mix in sugar, flour and lemon juice until well blended. Pour over hot baked crust and bake for 20 more minutes. Remove from oven and cool. Dust with powdered sugar and cut into squares.

Colorado Tea Cakes

A tasty snack with tea, coffee, or punch. For home, office, wedding receptions, showers or any gathering.

1 cup BUTTER
1/2 cup POWDERED SUGAR
1 tsp. VANILLA
2 cups FLOUR

1/4 tsp. SALT
1/2 cup NUTS, chopped
POWDERED SUGAR,
for coating

Cream butter and sugar, add vanilla. Gradually add flour and salt. Add chopped nuts. Roll into small balls. Place on ungreased cookie sheet. Bake in 350 degree oven for 30 to 40 minutes until slightly browned. When partially cooled, roll in powdered sugar.

Yield: 35-40 tea cookies.

Raisin Spice Bars

1/2 cup RAISINS	1/2 tsp. BAKING SODA
1/2 cup WATER	1/2 tsp. CINNAMON
1 stick MARGARINE	1/2 tsp. NUTMEG
2/3 cup SUGAR	1/4 tsp. CLOVES
1 cup FLOUR	1 EGG

Simmer raisins in 1/2 cup water until plumped. Drain off water, saving 2 tablespoons. Melt margarine in saucepan; add 2 tablespoons of raisin water. Remove from heat and add sugar, blending well. Stir in flour, baking soda and spices. Add egg and beat well. Add raisins and stir lightly to combine. Pour into a greased, deep-sided cookie sheet. Bake at 350 degrees for 20 to 25 minutes. Remove from pan immediately. Do not stack.

Yield: approximately 18 bars.

Easy Never Fail Holiday Fudge

"Christmas without fudge is like no Christmas at all. Most of my friends love chocolate. With the busy schedule everyone seems to have nowadays this recipe is very easy and quick but, most important, very delicious." Amelia V. Smith, Pueblo

1 can (14 oz.) SWEETENED CONDENSED MILK
1 pkg. (12 oz.) SEMI-SWEET CHOCOLATE CHIPS
1 1/2 tsp. VANILLA
1 cup WALNUTS or PECANS, chopped

Put the sweetened condensed milk in a double boiler with the entire package of semi-sweet chocolate chips. Stir until chocolate chips melt. Remove from heat and add vanilla and chopped nuts. Pour into a greased 9 x 13 pan. Cool. Cut into 24 squares.

Chocolate Truffles

"The best truffles I ever had were from a store in Iowa. The first time I tasted them, I was determined I'd make some equally as good. This is the result of trial and error for many years. They are actually better! I do order my chocolate from that store. I give these in decorative tins as presents at Christmas." Dianne Eschman, Telluride

A candy thermometer is essential for this recipe.

3 1/3 cups HEAVY CREAM
14 Tbsp. UNSALTED BUTTER
Approximately 4 lbs. good quality
     SEMI-SWEET CHOCOLATE, broken into pieces
GRAND MARNIER, KAHLUA or AMARETTO
COCOA
3 lbs. BITTERSWEET CHOCOLATE (again, good quality)
     for dipping
VEGETABLE SHORTENING

Put cream and butter into saucepan. Let butter melt over medium heat then, stirring all the while, turn up heat and let the cream come just to a boil. Turn off the heat, add the semi-sweet chocolate and stir until it is completely melted. Continue stirring until the mixture thickens and cools somewhat. Divide mixture into separate bowls (depending on the number of different flavors you wish to make) and add liqueur, a tablespoon at a time, until desired flavor level is reached. Cover, place in refrigerator and allow to thicken overnight. Stir 3 or 4 times as it cools.

To form truffles, scoop up portions of the chocolate with a spoon. Dust lightly with cocoa and form into balls. Place balls on baking sheets and return to refrigerator immediately to recool.

Melt bittersweet chocolate with shortening in the proportions of 12 ounces of chocolate to 2 tablespoons plus 2 teaspoons of shortening. Melt enough to dip all truffles.

(Continued next page)

Tempering:

Heat mixture to 108 degrees, stirring constantly with a rubber spatula. When chocolate reaches 108 degrees, remove from heat. Stir until chocolate cools to 85 degrees. Continue stirring and scraping until mixture reaches 80 degrees. Keep mixture at this temperature, stirring constantly, for 10 minutes. This is important to develop the crystals necessary for the glossy finish. Rewarm the chocolate to 86 degrees — hold there for 5 minutes before dipping. Keep chocolate at 86 degrees for the entire dipping process. Remove balls from refrigerator, allow to come to room temperature. Dip each ball in chocolate to coat. Place on wax paper or cookie sheet. Refrigerate again for 2 hours. Store in plastic containers, with wax papers between the layers to prevent sticking. Keep in a cool place.

Yield: approximately 6 dozen.

Note: To identify the different flavors of truffles, put something on the top of each while still warm (i.e. an almond slice on the top of the Amaretto ones).

Sleigh Bell Cookies

People of Colorado enjoy winter sports: skiing, skating, snowmobiling and so on. They take these cookies with them in their pockets for an energy snack.

1 cup BUTTER
2 cups BROWN SUGAR
3 EGGS
1/4 cup HONEY
1 tsp. BRANDY EXTRACT
1 tsp. VANILLA
3 1/2 cups FLOUR
1 tsp. BAKING SODA
1 tsp. CINNAMON
1/2 tsp. CLOVES
1/2 tsp. NUTMEG
1 cup WHITE RAISINS
1 cup DATES, chopped
1 cup FRUIT CAKE FRUIT MIX
1 cup NUTS, chopped
1/4 cup LEMON JUICE

Cream butter and sugar. Add eggs, one at a time, beating until fluffy. Add honey and extracts. Blend until smooth. Mix dry ingredients together. Add and mix until all is well blended. Add raisins, dates, fruit, and nuts. Add lemon juice last. Drop by spoonfuls onto cookie sheet. Bake at 350 degrees for 20 minutes or until golden.

Yield: 6 dozen.

Marshmallow Cream Fudge

1 jar MARSHMALLOW CREAM
1 1/2 cups SUGAR
2/3 cup EVAPORATED MILK
1/4 cup BUTTER or MARGARINE
1/4 tsp. SALT
1 pkg. (12 oz.) CHOCOLATE CHIPS
1/2 cup NUTS
1 tsp. VANILLA

Combine marshmallow cream, sugar, evaporated milk, butter and salt. Bring to a full boil stirring constantly over moderate heat. Boil 5 minutes stirring constantly. Remove from heat. Add chocolate chips and stir until melted. Stir in nuts and vanilla. Pour into greased 8-inch square pan. Chill until firm.

Yield: about 2 1/4 pounds.

Pizzelle Cookies

You'll need a pizzelle iron to make these delicious and easy cookies for the holidays.

6 EGGS
1 1/2 cups SUGAR
1 cup MARGARINE, melted
2 Tbsp. VANILLA or ANISE or LEMON EXTRACT
3 1/2 cups FLOUR
4 tsp. BAKING POWDER

Beat eggs and gradually add sugar. Beat until smooth. Add melted margarine and extract. Sift together flour and baking powder. Add to mixture a little at a time. Heat pizzelle iron. Pour a small amount of batter onto the iron. Remove when light brown.

Pumpkin Bars

"As a child on the farm in the 1940s and 1950s, we had lots of pumpkins and squash and hunted for many ways to use them. Not everyone liked pie or baked squash, so we looked for other ways to use the things we had. Down through the years, we revised this recipe by taking out the lard and using oil instead. We have also decreased the sugar. This is served warm at Christmas to guests. It can be frozen and keeps well for months. Colorado is well-known for pumpkins, and not all are used for Jack-0-Lanterns." Ethel Montgomery, Lamar

3/4 cup OIL
1 1/2 cups SUGAR
4 EGGS
1 tsp. VANILLA
1/4 tsp. BLACK WALNUT FLAVORING
2 cups canned PUMPKIN
2 cups FLOUR
1 tsp. SODA
1 tsp. BAKING POWDER
1 tsp. CINNAMON
1/2 cups NUTMEATS
1 cup PRUNES, cut in small pieces and floured

Combine in order except nuts and prunes. Mix well and then stir them in. This recipe can be used as bars, loaves or muffins. Bake in a 13 x 19 pan at 350 degrees for 40 minutes for bars; bake 25 minutes for muffins; and 60 minutes for a loaf. Frost with cream cheese frosting or sprinkle with powdered sugar. The prunes are added for extra sweetness and nutrition.

Yield: 24 bars.

Fattigmann

A delightful, crispy food attractive at any party.

1 Tbsp. BUTTER, melted
1/3 cup CREAM
1/3 cup SUGAR
1 tsp. SALT
6 EGG YOLKS
1/2 tsp. ground CARDAMOM or NUTMEG
1 Tbsp. grated LEMON RIND
1 3/4 - 2 cups all purpose FLOUR
FAT for deep frying
POWDERED SUGAR

Blend together butter, cream, sugar, salt and egg yolks. Beat until light and fluffy. Add cardamom or nutmeg and lemon rind. Gradually add flour to form a stiff dough. Roll out dough, a fourth at a time on a floured surface, until paper thin. With pastry wheel or sharp knife, cut into strips about 1 1/2-inch wide. Then cut diagonally at 4-inch intervals. Make 2-inch slit lengthwise in center of each piece, then slip one end through slit. Fry in hot deep fat (350 degrees) until delicately browned, about one minute on each side. Turn and remove with slotted spoon. Drain on absorbent paper. Sprinkle with powdered sugar.

Yield: 60 to 70.

Christmas Wreaths

"Tiring of mixing Christmas cookie dough for my five young daughters to roll out, cut with cookie cutters and decorate, and needing a few more festive cookies, I made this recipe which they enjoyed shaping and decorating." Ruth H. McGraw, Estes Park

3 Tbsp. MARGARINE
1/2 cup LIGHT CORN SYRUP
1 drop GREEN FOOD COLORING
3 Tbsp. SUGAR
3 1/2 cups CORNFLAKES
RED CINNAMON CANDIES, TINY SILVER BALLS, RAINBOW MIX DECORATIONS

Cook first four ingredients over medium heat, stirring constantly. Cook for five minutes. Add cornflakes. Stir until well-coated. Using a buttered tablespoon, measure out 18 mounds. With buttered hands, form each mound into a 2-inch diameter wreath. Decorate wreaths as desired with red cinnamon candies, tiny silver balls, and rainbow mix decorations.

Yield: 18 wreaths.

Christmas Sugar Cookies

Simple and satisfying, sugar cookies are the ultimate Christmas cookie.

1 cup SHORTENING
2 cups SUGAR
1 EGG
1 cup MILK (approximately)
1 tsp. BAKING SODA
1 tsp. LEMON EXTRACT
3 - 4 cups FLOUR

Cream the shortening and sugar. Put the egg in 1-cup measuring cup and add milk. Add baking soda and blend into creamed mixture. Add lemon extract and blend in flour. Roll out dough on a lightly floured board to 1/8 inch thickness. Cut with a cookie cutter in your favorite Christmas shapes and place on an ungreased baking sheet. Sprinkle with sugar and bake at 375° for 8-10 minutes until lightly browned.

Note: For variation, omit sprinkle of sugar and after cookies cool frost with colored icing.

Holiday Spritz

2 1/3 cups sifted FLOUR
1/2 tsp. SALT
1 cup MARGARINE

2/3 cups SUGAR
1 EGG, beaten
1 tsp. VANILLA

Sift together flour and salt. Stir margarine and sugar until well blended. Add beaten egg and vanilla; beat well. Stir in flour mixture. Press dough through cookie press onto ungreased cookie sheet. Bake at 400 degrees until lightly browned on edges for 8-10 minutes. Cool on wire racks.

Yield: 4 dozen.

Christmas Fruit Bars

"This is our favorite cookie recipe for the holidays and it was a must requested by my two daughters. Every year my girls would deliver these cookies to Santa at Silverton's Town Square—even when they were in college. I am now a great grandmother and these cookies are still in demand." Marge Bell, Silverton.

1 cup SUGAR	1 tsp. BAKING SODA
1/4 cup BUTTER	1/2 tsp. CINNAMON
1/4 cup SHORTENING, softened	1/2 tsp. NUTMEG
1 EGG	1 cup RAISINS
1 Tbsp. grated ORANGE RIND	1 cup CANDIED FRUIT
1/4 cup ORANGE JUICE	1/2 cup PECANS, chopped
2 1/2 cups sifted FLOUR	POWDERED SUGAR

Cream sugar, butter and shortening. Add egg and orange rind. Mix well. Stir in orange juice. Sift flour, soda, cinnamon and nutmeg and stir in. With hands, mix in raisins, fruit pieces and nuts. Divide dough in half. On a cloth covered board dusted with powdered sugar, roll out each half into a 7 x 12 rectangle. Cut into 6 x 7 strips. Bake on lightly greased cookie sheet, 10 to 12 minutes in a 400 degree oven. While still warm, stripe bars with **Powdered Sugar Icing.** Cut baked strips into bars.

Note: If raisins or fruit are dry, rinse with hot water. DRAIN WELL before using. Dab with paper towel or dough will be too sticky to handle.

Powdered Sugar Icing

1 1/2 Tbsp. BUTTER
1 cup POWDERED SUGAR
1/2 tsp. VANILLA
Approximately 1 1/2 Tbsp. MILK

Combine all ingredients. Add more sugar if needed.

Cream Candy

This candy is best if aged. Make it at Thanksgiving and serve it at Christmas.

6 cups SUGAR
1 bottle DARK CORN SYRUP
1 1/2 pt. WHIPPING CREAM
VANILLA to taste
1 1/2 lb. NUTMEATS

Heat sugar, corn syrup and whipping cream in a heavy saucepan until mixture reaches soft ball stage. Add vanilla. Beat for a long time, beginning with an electric mixer and then stirring by hand as it becomes harder. (You may have to recruit a strong man, or at least bring in the reliefs.) When ridges start forming in mixture, add nutmeats. Pour into two 9 x 12 cake pans. Allow to cool and cut into squares. Store in an airtight container.

Peanut Brittle

An old-time recipe for peanut brittle — an absolute must for the Christmas season.

1 1/2 cups SUGAR
1 3/4 cups GOLDEN CORN SYRUP
2/3 cup COLD WATER
1/2 lb. UNSALTED PEANUTS
1 Tbsp. BUTTER
3/4 tsp. BAKING SODA
1 tsp. WATER

Boil sugar, corn syrup and cold water until it forms a hard ball. Add peanuts and butter and stir until a brown color. Then add the baking soda dissolved in a teaspoon of water. Mix well and pour into a buttered shallow pan. When cool, break into pieces.

Sugar Spiced Pecans

"This was my mother's recipe. She always served these candies at Christmas time when I was a little girl. Now we serve them at the Castle Marne during the Christmas season at Teatime." Diane Peiker, Castle Marne Bed & Breakfast, Denver

1/2 cup BUTTER
1 cup BROWN SUGAR
1 1/2 cups GRANULATED SUGAR
2 Tbsp. CINNAMON
2 tsp. each ALLSPICE AND NUTMEG
1 tsp. GROUND CLOVES
3/4 cup LIGHT CORN SYRUP
1/2 cup ORANGE JUICE
Zest from 1 ORANGE and 1 LEMON (optional)
2 pounds PECANS
Small pkg. RED HOTS®

Combine all ingredients except pecans and Red Hots in a large sauce pan. Stir over medium heat until dissolved. Add pecans and cook for ten minutes, stirring constantly. Spread onto large cookie sheet and bake at 250 degrees until liquid bubbles. Remove from oven and cool five minutes. Coat thoroughly with granulated sugar and sprinkle Red Hots over nuts, making certain that they get stuck to the nuts. Store at room temperature in open container.

Yield: 2 pounds.

The Castle Marne

The Castle Marne Bed & Breakfast is located in one of Denver's most historic neighborhoods. Built in 1889, this grand mansion was designed by architect William Lang, who also designed the home of the "Unsinkable Molly Brown."

Index

Christmas in Colorado Cook Book

Recipe Contributors

Thank You!

Selected art throughout this book by Steve Parker

 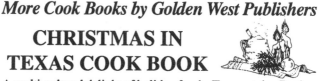

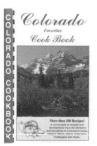

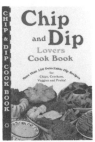

ORDER BLANK

GOLDEN WEST PUBLISHERS

☼ 4113 N. Longview Ave. • Phoenix, AZ 85014

602-265-4392 • **1-800-658-5830** • FAX 602-279-6901

Qty	Title	Price	Amount
	Apple Lovers Cook Book	6.95	
	Arizona Cook Book	5.95	
	Best Barbecue Recipes	5.95	
	Chili-Lovers' Cook Book	5.95	
	Chip and Dip Lovers Cook Book	5.95	
	Christmas in Arizona Cook Book	8.95	
	Christmas in Colorado Cook Book	8.95	
	Christmas in New Mexico Cook Book	8.95	
	Christmas in Texas Cook Book	8.95	
	Christmas in Washington Cook Book	8.95	
	Citrus Lovers Cook Book	6.95	
	Colorado Favorites Cook Book	5.95	
	Cowboy Cartoon Cook Book	5.95	
	Eating Inn Style! Colorado Cook Book	8.95	
	Pecan-Lovers' Cook Book	6.95	
	Quick-n-Easy Mexican Recipes	5.95	
	Recipes for a Healthy Lifestyle	6.95	
	Salsa Lovers Cook Book	5.95	
	Tequila Cook Book	7.95	
	Wholly Frijoles! The Whole Bean Cook Book	6.95	
	Add $2.00 to total order for shipping & handling		**$2.00**

☐ My Check or Money Order Enclosed. . . . . $ _____

☐ MasterCard ☐ VISA

(Payable in U.S. funds)

Acct. No. _____ Exp. Date _____

Signature _____

Name _____ Telephone _____

Address _____

City/State/Zip _____

Call or write for FREE catalog

11/95   MasterCard and VISA Orders Accepted ($20 Minimum)

Xmas CO

This order blank may be photo-copied.